75¢

WRAPPED IN FABRIQUÉ™

Wrapped in FABRIQUÉ™

THE NEW MAGIC OF FABRIC EMBELLISHMENT, MACHINE EMBROIDERY, AND APPLIQUÉ

GLENDA D. SPARLING

RANITA CORPORATION
EUGENE, OREGON

Ranita Corp. Publications has strived to provide the reader with the highest level of quality in each facet of this publication. In this regard, we expressly wish to acknowledge the following individuals and companies whose work, assistance, and support made this project a publication we can proudly present to you — our valued reader.

Illustrations by: Kate Pryka
Design by: Gwen Rhoads
Desktop publishing by: Shirley Walker-Combs
Photography by: Northwestern Photographics
Copyediting by: Paul Wade
Production management and coordination by: Wesley Sparling
Pre-print production and printing by:
Koke Printing - Eugene, OR, USA
Creative consulting by:
Jenny Anastas & Margaret Lawtie - Perth, Australia
Special acknowledgment and thanks to
Madeira Marketing Ltd. USA, a leading manufacturer of high quality specialty threads, trims, and braids.

First printing: April 1994
Second printing: June 1994

Also available from Ranita Corporation:
Publications, patterns, and videos on pattern fitting and designing.

Published in Eugene, Oregon, USA by Ranita Corporation
P.O. Box 5698
Eugene, OR 97405-0698
PH: (503) 344-0422   FAX: (503) 344-3944

ISBN 0-9640438-0-7

FOREWORD

Glenda Sparling has traveled thousands of miles to teach Sure-Fit Designs'™ special brand of fitting and sewing to scores of information-hungry audiences around the world. Because of her in-person rapport and dialogue with their many customers, she is in a unique position to anticipate their hesitations and troubleshoot their obstacles. She does both well in "Wrapped in Fabriqué™."

Her refreshing "no-right-no-wrong" attitude is inspiring and contagious: that we are each talented, and yes, creative, and that, indeed, there are no mistakes but simply new adventures in creativity. I totally agree.

You'll also enjoy the book's straightforward, easy-to-follow organization. Each chapter covers another aspect of embellishment (tucking, appliqué, puckering, scrunching, and woven magic, to name a few), so dive in however, wherever, and whenever the creative spirit moves you. Instructions are enhanced by the enlightening work of Kate Pryka, undoubtedly one of the best illustrators in the business.

As Glenda says, "free yourself to create," drawing inspiration from the project photography and tips within. Beautiful results — garments, decor, crafts — are in the offing, as are wonderful journeys in self-satisfaction and expression.

Gail Brown, *Author*

Well-known sewing journalist and author of "Gail Brown's All-New Instant Interiors," "Innovative Sewing," "Innovative Serging," and seven other books

CONTENTS

CHAPTER ONE

CREATIVITY WITH FABRIQUÉ™

W ELCOME TO WRAPPED IN FABRIQUÉ™!

How wonderful it is to not have to be rigid and structured. Whatever you do is *right*. There are no mistakes.

   With this thought in mind, let me relate to you an experience that I had many years ago while I was substitute teaching for a third-grade class. The project during this particular class was for the students to color in butterflies. One student came to me and asked what color to use. I said she could use any color she wished. She was obviously distraught with that answer, so I told her to use blue. When the next student asked what color to use, I said to use red. On it went until I had instructed each student on which color to use. All of a sudden I realized there was a very

2

negative hub-bub in the room. When I asked what the problem was, a little boy said, "You told her to use red, him to use blue, her to use yellow, and me to use gray." I asked why is there a problem? "Our regular teacher always tells us to use the same color," he said.

Aren't you glad you aren't in that class? You have the capability to free yourself to create whatever you want, use whatever color you like, texturize your fabric with any technique you desire, and use whatever threads, trims, beads, or cords you wish. Your resulting project will be different from mine — truly exciting and unique.

Don't be concerned with what you are doing to the point that you worry about doing it right or wrong or even that it might be like someone else's. Eliminate any concern about "making mistakes." Often times, if you let the undesirable experiences happen, you discover some new and joyous aspect which could be applied to another project. We all may create things we don't like initially, but this can lead to new discoveries of what we do like. Some of us have come through an educational system where we were taught that there is only one correct way of accomplishing the goal. Hopefully, you have learned that this is not always the case. Even though it is sometimes difficult to break out of the "must do" mold, when you do you begin creating your own procedures, systems, and expressions of ideas, the rewards are truly limitless.

This book is about realizing your personal creativity. I sincerely hope that **Wrapped in Fabriqué**™ will not only teach you a variety of fabric manipulation techniques and give you creative options, but also will inspire your creativity and fill you with excitement. In accomplishing this, your sense of self-worth will increase, and most importantly your interest and fun with Fabriqué™ projects will expand to ever-higher goals. You will become truly "wrapped" in the ideas expressed throughout this book!

Inspiration

Traveling internationally for over 11 years has been both challenging and rewarding for me. Most people will easily identify with the challenges of business travel involving different countries, cities, people, cultures, and business attitudes. Clearly there have been times when thoughts of home where my own bed, kitchen, and family are have been very compelling. However, there has been one particular benefit that stands out from all the challenges. Simply, that is the free flow of information expressed by people excited to share their ideas, concepts, and techniques.

I have had the distinctive pleasure of meeting many talented, creative people during my travels who have greatly added to my reservoir of knowledge. Two women in particular—Jenny Anastas and Margaret Lawtie from Perth, Western Australia — have greatly impacted my interest and peaked my curiosity. It is with memories of the many stimulating conversations with these two lovely ladies that this book is written.

Jenny Anastas – Perth, Australia – Creative Consultant

As a result of the free-flowing exchange of ideas, concepts, and techniques between Jenny, Margaret, and I, an exciting electricity usually sparked our creativity. From this electric creativity the concept of Fabriqué™ emerged.

Often we discussed how human culture is so large and complex that we are led to believe that creativity and talent are qualities other people possess. Certainly the very idea of being creative, or stated another way, being different from what other people are doing, can be intimidating. Oftentimes, rather than face rejection or failure, we don't even try. In reality, all thinking people are endowed with the ability to choose between likes and dislikes. From this reservoir within our conscious mind, creativity starts its journey to full development. Once a person frees the restraints of culture, has the courage to try something different from what other people are doing, and allows creativity to develop and grow, an exciting electricity will fill your every pore. With encouragement from curiosity, self-expression, and imagination, fulfillment and art can grace our lives.

Margaret Lawtie – Perth, Australia – Creative Consultant

Some of you will be immediately inspired when your eyes light upon some aspect of your daily living. Others of us need help to let our creative thoughts flow. Let me suggest looking to your environment to help inspire your thoughts. I'll explain.

Glenda Sparling – Eugene, Oregon – author and President of Ranita Corporation

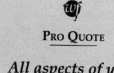

PRO QUOTE

All aspects of your environment are natural resources for developing your creative ideas.

On a recent overseas flight, as we were looking at the clouds below us, my husband mentioned that it would be great to recreate the fluffiness of the clouds in a form of fabric embellishment. As I sit at my desk and look towards the trees and their changing fall colors, I see nature's color patterns and consider their application in color mixing with fabric. In another incident, I was staring at a woman's wool sweater that had many raised, knitted ridges on it. This was my inspiration for developing the chapter on "Tubes 'n Tunnels." Look to nature; look to those around you; look in magazines, catalogues, greeting cards, and art of all types and let your imagination flow. I think you will be amazed that once you let the creative process begin, you don't have to rely solely on your imagination.

"Patience Is A Virtue"

We all know this well-worn phrase. It definitely applies when you are doing many different projects — not just with fabric manipulation and embellishment.

The techniques offered in this book are easy to do, however, some of them require more time than others. Sometimes, when everything seems to be going along just fine, your thread breaks, you run out of bobbin thread, a needle breaks, or the fabric pops out of your hoop. Don't despair! Take a big breath and know that this happens to everyone. You might even consider putting on some relaxing music each time you sit down to sew. Subliminally it could make you more relaxed. Don't fight the project. If threads keep breaking, change the needle, change the thread tension, or focus on a different aspect of the project and return to the frustrating component later.

Please enjoy yourself and know that the outcome will be beautiful and rewarding. When folks stop me and ask if I made a particular item, and they give me lots of compliments, I know my few frustrating times were worth it.

What Is "Wrapped In Fabriqué™?"

Fabriqué™ is the new magic of machine embroidery, appliqué, and fabric embellishment. In a compact definition, **Wrapped in Fabriqué™** is a book of process, where the components of a uniquely designed, embellished, and sewn garment are explained individually. It is a book written for the home seamstresses and fabric enthusiasts.

This comfortable jacket was sewn from a beautiful Italian wool. Even though the fabric already had a woven-in surface textural design, I knew it could be further enhanced with Fabriqué™ techniques to make it a truly "one-of-a-kind" garment.

PRO QUOTE

Wrapped in Fabriqué™ *is a book of process, where the components of a uniquely designed, embellished and sewn garment are explained individually. It's all about the new magic of machine embroidery, fabric manipulation and appliqué.*

What I have done in **Wrapped in Fabriqué**™ is offered you a book of manipulation processes and techniques, in a "how-to" format. Once you discover the process of the individual techniques and ideas represented here, you will have the capability to use the result in any project you want and as creatively as you want. The sewing machine becomes the brush, the fabric becomes the canvas, and Fabriqué™ becomes the technique. The result — a unique, one-of-a-kind garment of stunning beauty which expresses your individual creativity.

However, for your benefit and as an impetus to get your creativity underway, I have provided "The Project Page" which you will find at the end of chapters 4 through 14. The Project Page will illustrate and describe how a particular technique covered in the chapter has been used in a finished garment. Your personal deviations from these suggested projects is not only allowed but heartily encouraged. Remember, it is your creative interpretations of the technique and its project application that will make your garment truly unique for you.

Even though you can use these techniques on any project, the main intent of **Wrapped in Fabriqué**™ is to create wearable clothing. However, if you wish to make clothing accessories, soft home furnishings or wall hangings, that choice is yours. The techniques of Fabriqué™ lend themselves well to these ideas also.

Remember to experiment and enjoy yourself. The ultimate goal is to be creative, and keep in mind that it does not matter what you do — it is all right whatever the outcome.

CHAPTER TWO

KNOW THE TERMS

IT WOULD BE A WISE IDEA TO TAKE SOME TIME, read over this chapter about getting to know the terms, and become familiar with them. Many of these terms will be frequently repeated throughout the coming chapters. If you have a general understanding of what the term means, it will make understanding and comprehending the described techniques and processes that much easier. Know that this information is here for you and feel free to refer back to this chapter at any time.

This red, matador jacket has been constructed from douppioni silk. Cable stitching, couching, and regular straight stitches embellish all areas of the front and back.

Pro Quote

Being familiar with these terms and their meanings will simplify your Fabriqué™ experience.

Background Fabric: Fabric which becomes the base for the applied appliqué or design work. Unlike backing fabric, background fabric will be visible in the final project.

Backing Fabric: Fabric which becomes the support for other fabrics to be attached onto. It is not visible on the completed work because the entire surface becomes completely covered.

Cable Stitching: When threads are too heavy, bulky, or textured to be threaded on the top of the machine, they are wound on the bobbin. The design is then stitched with the right side of the fabric *face down*. The bobbin tension is loosened so the thread will pull through smoothly. Alternately, it is advisable to purchase a separate bobbin case and loosen the tension permanently so that you do not need to interfere with the tension of the normal bobbin case. See Chapter 12

Concertina Tucking: A technique used in pin tucking — tucking first on the right side, then on the wrong side, then continuing this process. See Chapter 10.

Cornelly Stitch: This is a machine stitch pattern that moves and curves all around forming a continuous line of stitching; however, no stitch will ever touch a previous stitch. If your machine does not have this stitch pattern, you can freehand stitch a similar pattern. This is often referred to as a "stippling" stitch, particularly by quilters.

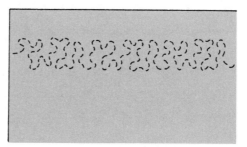

Couching: Lay threads, yarns, braids, or cords on surface of fabric and hand or machine stitch over the top to secure them to the fabric. It is easier to stitch when the cord is held up at a 45° angle in front of the needle while the machine stitches over top of the cord. You can use any type of zigzag stitch (or certain types of decorative stitches like a serpentine or cornelly stitch) to stitch over the cord/braid. To eliminate puckering, it is best to stabilize the background fabric using either a tear–away stabilizer or a hoop. See Chapter 12.

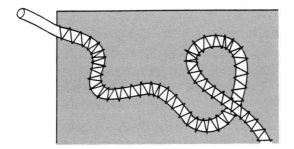

Dribbling: This is a variation of cable stitching. The decorative thread or lightweight yarn is wound on the bobbin, but rather than going through the loosened bobbin thread tension, the thread bypasses the tension slot/gauge and goes directly up through the machine's throat plate. See Chapter 12.

Fabric Puckering: This is a form of freehand embroidery that does not use a hoop. Fabric is pulled in, puckered up, and molded as you *scribble* stitch. See Chapter 6.

Fringing: Creating a fringed edge on a strip of fabric. Choose a suitable fabric that will fray or fringe easily. Straight stitch (or tight zigzag) on fabric at desired width away from raw edge following the grain of the fabric. Pull away fibers parallel to stitching, leaving the perpendicular fibers free to form the fringe. See Chapter 8.

Mélange: Creation of fabric using a water–soluble stabilizer, threads, yarns, and fabric bits. See Chapter 11.

Metalfil Needle: A large eyed needle. Frequently used when stitching metallic and rayon threads to help prevent splitting, shredding, and thread breakage.

Mixed Media: When more than one medium is utilized to create the finished piece, (for instance, use of silk fabric, gold thread, sequins, and/or ribbons in an artistic expression.)

Pin Tuck: A raised ridge of fabric is formed by using a twin (double) needle. The two top threads are gently pulled together by the single bobbin thread, thereby forming the fabric tuck on the top of the fabric's surface. See Chapter 10.

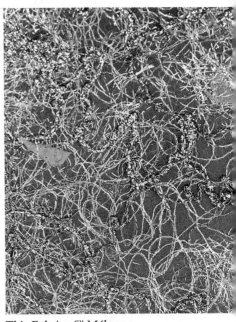

This Fabriqué™ Mélange technique is a very simple one to accomplish. All details of this fabric creation process are clearly described in Chapter 11.

Satin Stitch: This is a tight, compact zigzag stitch. The stitch length is set very short (.3 to .4 mm), which packs the zigzag stitches close together. The stitch width is often set at 2.5 to 3.5 mm. See Chapter 4.

Satin Stitch Burst: Set machine for zigzag. Set the stitch length at .3 to .35 mm. Set the stitch width at 0. With the machine running at an even speed, gradually increase the stitch width to 3 mm and then stitch for a short distance. Then gradually decrease the stitch width to 0 again.

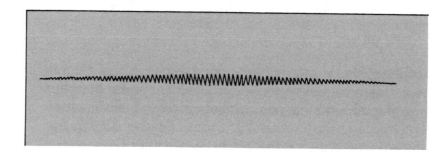

Scribble Stitching: It is done by freehand stitching in tight circles, semi–circles, and close figure "8's". Think of this as scribbling with stitches on the top of the fabric.

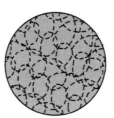

Scrunching: Manipulation of fabric by taking a two-dimensional surface, twisting, or stitching it, pressing, then releasing it to form uneven movement and a three-dimensional effect on the surface of the fabric. See Chapter 7.

This elegant Fabriqué™ jacket features not only scrunched appliqué, satin stitching, and decorative machine embroidery on each shoulder, but also gold and turquoise yarns have been twisted together and couched in cascading lines down each front panel.

Serpentine Stitch: The stitch gently sways or zigzags back and forth. It is also known as "three–step zigzag."

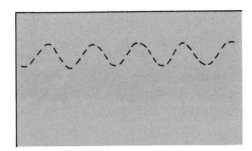

Solvy: A water–soluble gelatinous material used as a stabilizer. It will dissolve away completely in water. See Chapter 2 and 11.

Swing Couching: Using a very soft and pliable braid or trim (such as Madeira Carat, wool, or floss) and an embroidery stitch (such as a cornelly or serpentine stitch) place trim on the fabric and move the trim randomly from right to left as the machine stitches over the top. You can try various decorative machine stitch patterns to create your desired effect. See Chapter 12.

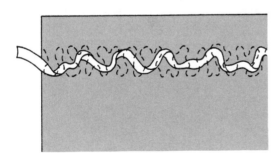

PRO QUOTE

When the thread begins shredding or skipping stitches, always change to a new needle.

Thread Wrapping: Set machine for close satin stitch. It can be done with the feed dog up and embroidery or appliqué foot on the machine. Loosen top tension or tighten bobbin tension so top thread wraps around the cord or four or five threads. Use same thread top and bobbin. Use a satin stitch wide enough for the needle to swing and miss the cord or threads. The cord or threads must be held taut behind and in front of the sewing foot and you must pull gently, evenly, and very slowly through it as you sew.

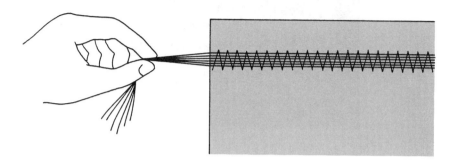

Tracing Vellum: A lightweight yet see-through and durable paper pattern–tracing medium. This is also useful as a pressing aide. See Resource List in the back of this book for purchasing information.

Vliesofix (Wonder Under): Australian trade name for paper–backed fusible webbing.

Wonder Under (Vliesofix): Trade name for a paper–backed fusible webbing product.

CHAPTER THREE

KNOW
THE
TOOLS
—
SUPPLIES &
EQUIPMENT
———

GETTING STARTED on your Fabriqué™ experience requires only some special tools and equipment. Most likely, you will find that you have much of this equipment and many of the supplies already in your sewing room. Check this chapter for a comprehensive mention of required items. Then, at the beginning of each chapter, a "Specific Materials and Supplies" list is given to you.

The Sure-Fit Designs™ pattern system offers a multitude of sizes and unlimited designing capabilities — a real plus for Fabriqué™.

Patterns

Most of the fabric manipulation techniques explained in **Wrapped in Fabriqué**™ are applied to some style of wearable garment — a vest, jacket, blouse, or coat. You can use whatever patterns you choose; however, the patterns that have been used throughout this book are from the Sure–Fit Designs™ pattern line. Sure–Fit Designs™ is a multisized pattern system. It is a reusable master pattern, with the flexibility to design any style of garment you wish and ideal for Fabriqué™ on projects. For more information regarding Sure–Fit Designs™ products, see the Resource List at the back of the book.

Whichever patterns you choose to work with, the design elements should be relatively simple — that is, those which have a minimum number of design lines, darts, or intricate pattern detail — because the fabric manipulations that you will do and that are applied to the garment will be the focus of attention. If you require simple bust darts, they can be incorporated into a manipulated section and often hidden from view. Simple princess lines can often be covered up with an appliquéd embellishment; however, it is best and easiest to keep these necessary fitting components to a minimum. Furthermore, you don't want to have a design feature interfering with the beautiful, creative work that you will do. Remember, when it comes to pattern choice — *the simpler the better!*

Additionally, you will find many pattern designs, shapes, and motifs in Chapter 16. Feel free to use these pattern shapes and ideas as you wish. You will find geometric shapes, abstract shapes, and realistic shapes for your use. Use them as-is, use portions of the designs, add to the shapes, and be as creative as you desire. Chapter 16 is intended to give you lots of ideas for different projects you may wish to do.

Your Sewing Machine

Most machines will be suitable; however, those with some decorative embroidery stitches are preferable. Even when using a machine that simply straight stitches and zigzags or that has limited stitch patterns, you will be able to accomplish almost all of the manipulation techniques and embellishment procedures described in this book. As you become accustomed to and proficient in freehand stitching and embroidery techniques, you will be able to add your own special variety of final decorative embellishments. With machines that have embroidery stitch capabilities, you will be able to use the machine's built–in, preprogrammed decorative stitches to complete the fabric embellishment. Make sure you clean and oil your machine prior to beginning a project because all types of threads — including metallics and rayons — create a lot of lint. Make sure you clean the machine well after each project. In fact, a good habit to get into is to dust the machine and remove lint buildup and to insert a new needle every time you sit down to sew. Try to keep the machine covered when not in use. Another suggestion is to wind six or seven bobbins full, then when these are used it will be time again to give your machine a thorough cleaning. A soft brush for removing lint and bits of fabric is handy to have. The care that you give your machine will give you positive rewards when it sews without "hiccups" most of the time. Just as you maintain your car, it is important for your machine to be maintained and regularly serviced by a qualified technician.

Machine Feet

Sewing machine feet come in brand-specific and generic-type models. Make sure the feet are compatible with your machine.

PRO QUOTE

You do not require a fancy computer model machine to do Fabriqué™.Basic machines will adequately sew any of the fabric manipulation techniques.

You should have on hand:

- The regular straight stitch and zigzag foot. This foot does normal sewing and does not have a wide channel or groove on the underside.

- An open–toed appliqué or embroidery foot has a wide groove or channel on the underside. This allows the tightly stitched satin stitch to ride smoothly underneath. If the front of the foot is completely open, then you can see what you are sewing. If your brand sewing machine does not have an open–toed appliqué foot, it is possible that you can have your sewing machine mechanic take out the center section of a regular embroidery foot.

groove

- A darning or freehand embroidery foot is recommended for freehand embroidery. Make sure you follow the machine instructions when attaching the foot. The spring action from this foot allows it to move up and down as the needle pierces the fabric. This prevents the fabric from riding up on the needle and eliminates skipped stitches. And, for some reason, it seems easier to remember to lower the presser bar when you have a foot attached to the machine. If the presser bar is not lowered before beginning to sew, you can end up with a tangled mass of threads in a very short space of time.

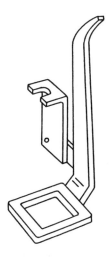

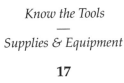
• A pin-tucking foot is used primarily with sewing pin tucks. See Chapter 10 for pin tucking details. This foot has multiple grooves on the underside which helps the pin tucks being stitched to be an equal distance apart. The more grooves the foot has, the closer the tucks will be together.

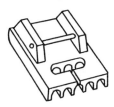

• A cording foot is useful when couching trims, braids, or yarns onto the fabric surface. See Chapter 12 for complete details. The foot often provides a hole in the front of the foot through which the cord is fed and therefore will feed automatically and evenly under the needle. Cording feet can also come with just one large groove on the underside which allows the cord to feed evenly under the presser foot.

18

Machine Needles

For good quality decorative stitching and satisfying results, always use new sharp needles. Needles don't have to break to no longer be of use. If they become dull, bent, or damaged, they will cause stitching problems. Because they are an integral part of the machine, make sure they are not dull. If the needle begins to make "noises" like it is forcing its way through the fabric, change it. If thread keeps skipping stitches, it could be the result of a dull needle. Change it. The average life of a needle is *eight sewing hours*. Consequently, it is very important to change the needle regularly. Also, make sure you purchase high-quality needles that are suited to your sewing machine. You will need a variety of needles depending on your fabric, thread choice, and desired outcome.

Have on hand:

- Sizes 10/70, 12/80, and 14/90 (10/12/14 refer to American sizes, 70/80/90 refer to European size)

- Metalfil needles. These metalfil needles have a larger eye. This allows the thread to pass through easier, particularly when stitching with metallic and rayon threads.

- Embroidery needles

- Twin (double) needle (2.0/80)

Scissors and Shears

The difference between scissors and shears is that shears are longer than 6" (15 cm). There are a multitude of different varieties, shapes, and styles of both. A general recommendation is that both need to be kept sharp. Constantly cutting anything will dull the blade with repeated use. When you find they are not doing the job you want them to do, have them sharpened. Quality often equates to long life and good value in length of use.

It is also useful to have a rotary cutter and cutting mat. These tools simplify the cutting of long, straight edges. The cutting mats are marked with dimensions, angles, and curved lines, which help to take the guess work out of making even cuts. Once again, the rotary blade dulls with continual usage. When it stops making clean cuts, change the blade.

Have on hand:

- A good pair of fabric shears

- A good pair of paper scissors

- Fine point, sharp embroidery scissors

- Thread snippers

- Rotary cutter and cutting mat

Fabric Stabilizers

Fabric stabilizers give the fabric extra body, which helps to prevent the fabric from puckering and bunching up. They also help to prevent stitch irregularities, skipped stitches, and thread breakage. It is safest to experiment on a sample before beginning your project so that you use the right stabilizer for the final project.

Have on hand:

- Fine- to medium-weight iron–on interfacing. When this is bonded to the fabric, it is not intended for it to be removed, so keep in mind it will make the final, embellished fabric somewhat heavier and stiffer.

- Double-sided bonding material (fusible webbing) with paper tear–away backing (for example, Wonder Under™ [Vliesofix]). This is nonwoven fusible web that has a paper backing. Once the web is adhered to the fabric or appliqué motif, the paper backing is removed, and the motif can be pressed onto the backing or background fabric.

- Tear–away stabilizer (for example, Stitch & Tear). This is nonwoven nonfusible product that can be pinned, basted, or held in place to the fabric while the decorative stitching is being done. When stitching is completed, the backing is simply torn away. That which remains between the stitch pattern will often wash away after the first couple of washings. A second type of tear–away stabilizer provides a nonwoven fusible product that is initially pressed and bonded to the backing or background fabric. This totally stabilizes the entire area. When stitching is completed, the

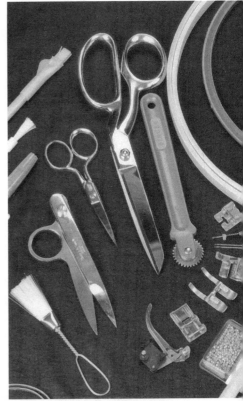

A variety of good quality scissors, shears, and cutting tools are essential in any sewing room. All of them need to be kept sharp to do the best job for you.

PRO QUOTE

The availability of bondable, tear–away fabric stabilizer makes appliqué work a breeze. New products enter the market frequently. Watch for them!

stabilizer is torn away. Save any large pieces if they have any of the bonding remaining on the paper backing for reuse on smaller projects, (for example, Totally Stable).

- Typewriter or computer paper. This can be used as a stabilizing medium. It goes between the throat plate and the fabric. It makes a plunking or plopping noise with each stitch. If this does not bother you, it is an acceptable stabilizer for some projects.

- Spray iron starch. One or more applications can be used depending on desired stiffness. Always test fabric sample before applying all over. This will wash out.

- Liquid stabilizer (for example, Perfect Sew). This is a thick gluelike consistency. It is applied to the fabric with a self–applicator or small paint brush. This can be used undiluted for a stiff, stabilized finish or watered down two parts water to one part stabilizer for a less-firm finish. This will wash out. Always do a test sample to check for color fastness and residual spotting.

- Water-soluble stabilizer (for example, Solvy, Melt–A–Way). This is a man made "spun alginate" solution. It is soft, stretchy, and quite fragile and tears easily. It should be stored away from humidity and moisture. It can be stitched into; however, this is generally only done in conjunction with using a hoop. When stitching is complete, wash well according to manufacturer's direction.

- Vanishing muslin. This resembles muslin fabric and is quite firm and easy to stitch into. It crumbles or disintegrates when pressed with a hot iron.

- Fusible fleece. This is a thin fleece (about $1/8$″ [.3 cm] thick) that has a fusible surface on one side. It is useful for stabilizing and great for creating padded, raised effects.

Hoops

Using an embroidery hoop can stabilize the fabric during stitching. Fabric will be stretched inside the hoop so that it will remain flat and tight while stitching through it. The hoop is an essential and integral part of freehand embroidery as it allows you to freely move the fabric under the needle while the machine is stitching. Using a hoop is also useful when stitching decorative, preprogrammed stitches, because it helps stop the fabric from pulling up and puckering.

Two types of embroidery hoops are available:

- Spring–loaded plastic hoop. The outer ring is plastic with a metal spring-tensioned ring inside. I find this type of hoop easier to maneuver while the fabric is being stitched. I also find this hoop easier to slide underneath the presser foot because the outer plastic ring is not as thick as a wooden hoop.

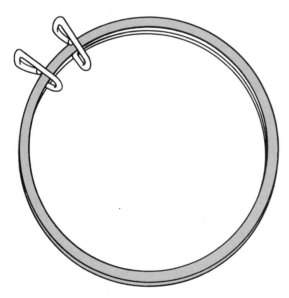

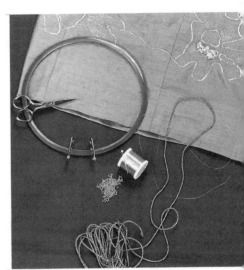

Embroidery hoops are commonly used to stretch and stabilize the fabric so that it does not pucker up on itself when being stitched. Margaret used a hoop to stabilize the silk as she freehand stitched the "fill-in" design on her evening gown.

- Wooden hoop. This has both the inner and outer ring made of wood (not bamboo). To prevent the fabric from slipping on the inside ring, I recommend that you wrap the inside ring with torn strips of cotton. Another method is to take cotton bias tape, press it open, wrap the inside ring with the tape, and secure the end with a touch of glue. When purchasing a wooden hoop, make sure it is thin enough to fit between the presser foot and the throat plate.

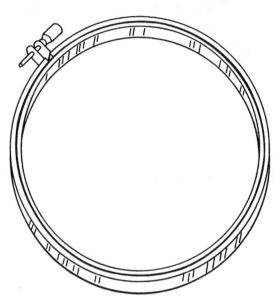

With either type, a hoop diameter of 7" (18 cm) to 10" (25 cm) is preferable. Hoops come in many diameters. It can be helpful to have two or three sizes of hoops available for varying project sizes.

Threads

There is a wide variety of threads for you to experiment with. Generally speaking, high-quality, brand-name threads equate to sewing satisfaction. Because less expensive off–brands often equate to being spun with shorter fiber lengths and therefore break more readily, quality becomes a wise investment. High-quality generally means that the thread has less "fuzz" on it. It will not break as often and can produce a more luxurious finish.

There are many specialty threads available that are particularly suited to machine embroidery and decorative stitching. A good 100% cotton or cotton-covered polyester thread is great for general garment construction and, if used for embroidery, will give a matte finish. Results may not be totally satisfactory, however. The rich color tones offered in rayon embroidery threads will give a rich, lustrous, and shiny appearance; however, because rayon is not a strong thread, it is not recommended for general construction. Metallic threads are available in various weights. The finer weights can be used on the top of the machine.

Having a good collection of high-quality, brand-name threads, yarns, cords, and trims will pay off when sewing as they tend to shred or break less frequently.

Heavier metallics can be wound on the bobbin and cable stitched or dribbled on the final project. They all add glitz and glamour to the final project.

- Madeira is one of the high-quality thread manufacturers and suppliers. Their threads come in a wide variety of brilliant colors and various weights. The #30 embroidery thread is a little heavier, it is more suitable for creating bolder designs and images. The #40 weight embroidery thread is somewhat finer and therefore recommended for more delicate designs, and free stitching. Cords, braids, and a variety of trims will add uniqueness to your finished garment. Madeira's Carat, a flat braid that comes in 2-mm and 4-mm widths, is excellent for couching over top of. Don't restrict yourself to just machine and fabric store threads. Knitting shops also have fine yarns that can add wonderful textural effects to your creative work.

And, just a note of caution, if the thread keeps breaking, try reducing the top thread tension, using a needle with a larger eye, using a *new* needle, or if you are working with metallic threads, use a new metalfil needle, and try sewing at a slower speed. It is also possible that the thread just simply is of poor quality — then you need to change threads.

Fabrics

In general, most any fabric is fair game. It can be manipulated, textured, and worked with in some manner to create Fabriqué™ effects. It is up to you to let your creativity evolve from the fabrics. I personally love the rich, vibrant colors of douppioni and Thai silk; however, on the other end of the continuum, more casual creations can evolve from denim, chambray, or cotton. See Chapter 14 where denim, lace, and metallic threads have been combined. You may also want a tone on tone effect where fabrics of different textures, but of similar colors are combined together. Or you may choose contrasting colors and textures, thereby creating a bolder, showy effect. Generally, plain fabrics will show the effects of the embellishment and be more dominant than embellishing on already patterned or surface-textured fabrics. Not all fabrics lend themselves well to all forms of treatments. For example, when you are scrunching fabric, natural fibers, or those blends that hold creases, will adapt better than 100% polyesters. Natural fibers like silks, rayons, and 100% cotton often work very well, whereas in the "Puckering" manipulation technique, see Chapter 6, you will want to work with soft drapy fabric of 100% polyester or a blend of poly with a natural fiber. Some of the

PRO QUOTE

The investment in good-quality, brand-name threads will mean less frustration when stitching. They tend to shred and break less often than off-brands.

PRO QUOTE

I recommend always stitching a test sample with the same fabrics, threads, yarns and trims that you will use on your final creation. It's better to be safe than sorry!

fabrics may require drycleaning and others can be hand or machine washed. Keep this in mind when blending fabrics together. If even one of them needs to be dry-cleaned, then the entire garment will need this cleaning process.

Sometimes you'll be able to use fabric in your "leftover" stash; other times you will need to purchase new and complimentary fabric pieces. In terms of fabric requirements, it is difficult to tell you how much fabric you will need. Sometimes the embellishment or manipulation technique will require a lot and other times a little yardage. It will also depend on whether you want to apply the technique to a localized area such as a yoke or a cuff, or whether you want to apply it to the entire garment.

With this in mind, I always recommend doing a *test sample* with the fabrics and threads you will use on your project. This gives you a feel for the technique, a visual impression of the final result, and helps you to gauge how much fabric you will need to manipulate in order to achieve the various techniques discussed in this book. It would be a good idea to record the size of the fabric piece you began with and what size it is when the process is completed. This will help you gauge how much you'll need for the entire project. When you know you want to manipulate fabric or add embellishments to a specific area of the final garment, always buy at least a half a yard more than you generally would and use the excess as your testing ground.

Also, I recommend that, when possible, all appliqué work, manipulating, and/or texturizing of the fabric is done first. Then you cut your final pattern or shape. Since this work can make the fabric move, shrink up, and do other strange things, always try to cut the final design or pattern last.

It's a good idea to save leftover fabric from other garment cuttings. Particularly save the shiny and glitzy fabrics like lamé, satins, or silks. You never know where they will come in useful. If you know someone who does dressmaking (particularly wedding gowns), have them collect their scraps for you — they could be your treasures.

You know the phrase "One man's trash is another man's treasure." Therefore, another source of potential and inexpensive fabric is to browse through the Goodwill, Salvation Army, or used clothing stores. You don't want the garment for the garment itself, but a silk or lamé blouse at $1.99 is far less expensive than yardage and, cut up, this could be just the highlight for you to manipulate and embellish with.

Those of you who tend to be "fabric-a-holics" will now be rewarded for your past purchasing insight. Check your stash. Lots of it will be very useful when doing these Fabriqué™ techniques.

Another suggestion is to sort your fabric stash. Use stackable bins, empty boxes, or even baskets and sort by fabric color tones. A box is also handy just for interfacing — one for specialty threads and yarns, or any other category that is relevant to your needs. This does not take much time to do and it makes it so much quicker and easier to find things when you're in a hurry or in the middle of the project.

Miscellaneous Supplies

- Teflon-coated appliqué mat — a square of teflon-coated material that prevents adhesives and fusibles from adhering to the iron.

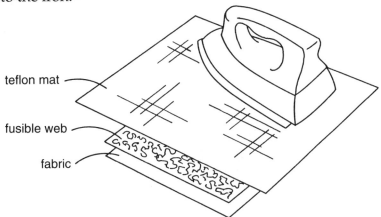

teflon mat

fusible web

fabric

- Tracing Vellum — This is a high-quality tracing paper, specially manufactured for your use in drawing off your master patterns. Available from Ranita Corporation in:

  - 10 yard rolls that are 24" wide or
  - 50 yard rolls that are 18" wide. See Resource List at the back of this book.

Not only is it used for tracing patterns, but also it's useful as a pressing medium.

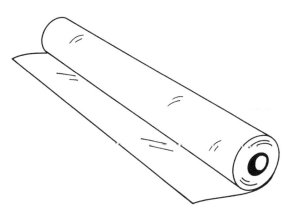

PRO QUOTE

What is one man's trash is another man's treasure. Keep all your scraps and anyone else's who will donate them to you.

• Iron and ironing board

• Vanishing fabric marking pen — for marking fabric designs and shapes

• Knitting needle or wooden skewer — for scrunching fabric and torn strips

• Polyester batting or fusible fleece (for example, Press–on Fleece®)

• Designing Stylus™ — This is an ingenious dressmaker's tool, that contains every curve representing your body — armholes, neckline, hip line, crotch curves, and more. This curved ruler is a necessary tool for easily and accurately drawing your personalized patterns. It is specially designed to work with *all* the Sure–Fit Designs™ patterns. See Resource List at the back of this book.

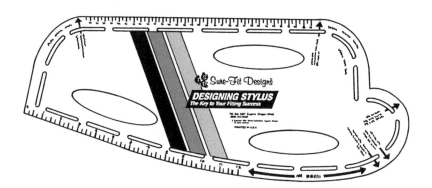

• French curve — a curved dressmaker's ruler

• Straight edge or yard stick

• Cardboard dressmaker's cutting board, pin board, or foam core board.

APPLIQUÉ: THE BASICS

Lᴇᴛ's ʙᴇɢɪɴ ᴡɪᴛʜ ᴀᴘᴘʟɪQᴜÉ. There are many books on the market about how to do appliqué work. I do not intend to greatly expand on that voluminous information; however, because many of the fabric manipulation and texturizing techniques that are described in this book are then appliquéd onto backing or background fabric, I will briefly cover the basic methods. As you review the basic elements of appliqué, you establish a solid foundation that opens the exciting world of **Wrapped in Fabriqué**™.

Appliqué means that different shapes of fabric are stitched onto a backing or background fabric either by hand or machine stitching. Since all of us appreciate the speed of our sewing machines, this chapter will focus on machine appliqué only. Machine appliqué is relatively quick to do and lends itself to various expressions of the craft.

Appliqué procedures can be used in wall hangings, soft furnishings, articles of apparel, and sewn pictures. Some of you will prefer to use existing patterns or shapes by which to cut your appliqué motif. Others of you will prefer to use your imagination and spontaneity to cut shapes and motifs in random designs and then stitch them to the backing or background fabric.

There are many different ways of preparing and doing appliqué. Some patterns and design shapes are stitched on the right side of the fabric. Other techniques require stitching from the wrong side. For some designs, the entire appliqué shape outline is drawn onto tear–away stabilizer or lightweight nonwoven interfacing first. Then the corresponding pieces of appliqué fabric are cut and are laid in place on the right side of the backing or background fabric and stitched down. Sometimes the appliqué shapes are assembled on the top of the backing or background fabric either in specific designs (as in creating recognizable forms like leaves, flowers, animals, etc.) or they are "shaped to the eye" and laid down randomly. These techniques are visually illustrated in the following sections Method 1 and 2. In either situation, they are stitched down to the backing or background fabric.

SPECIFIC MATERIALS AND SUPPLIES

- Fabric
- Thread
- Paper–backed fusible webbing
- Tear–away stabilizer
- Iron–on interfacing
- Typewriter or computer paper
- Embroidery foot or open–toed foot
- Appliqué mat
- Embroidery hoop
- Tracing vellum

Design Decisions

Decide on the design to be appliquéd. A lot of appliqué consists of precise shapes that have a specific corresponding area that they must be sewn to. If this is the case, the entire design area to be appliquéd should be drawn or transferred onto the backing or background fabric. One way to do this is to draw your final design on tracing vellum. You can transfer these design shapes to the fabric with dressmaker's chalk or tracing wheel. The more complex the design, the more likely you should give each piece of the design a number. This number then relates to the appliqué fabric and shape that is to be sewn in that specific area. A slight variation of this numbering process was used in the fuchsia–black–gold vest construction found in Chapter 15.

Or if your final design is much more random, you may not need to transfer the original design to the background fabric. Rather, you will randomly cut the appliqué shape and randomly place it at will on the background fabric. This random placement technique is what was used on the green silk blouse shown on color plate #13.

Applying the Appliqué

There are many ways of doing appliqué. Here, two basic methods are reviewed.

Method 1

1. Draw or trace the mirror image of your appliqué shape onto the paper side of paper–backed fusible webbing.

2. Cut out the shape leaving a ½" (1.3 cm) margin.

½" margin

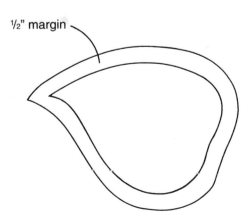

PRO QUOTE

Small, very sharp, very pointed embroidery scissors are a worthwhile investment when doing any kind of appliqué and embroidery stitching.

30

3. Press fusible side of shape to wrong side of appliqué fabric. Don't forget to use your appliqué mat between fabric and iron.

4. Trim away excess fabric and ½" (1.3 cm) margin.

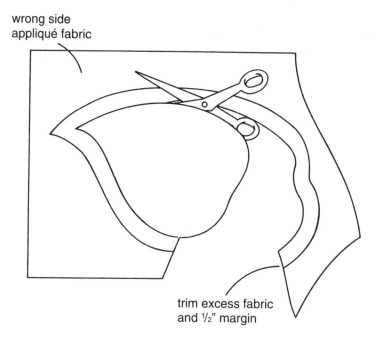

wrong side
appliqué fabric

trim excess fabric
and ½" margin

5. Remove the paper backing from the shape. Turn the shape over and press the fusible web side onto the right side of the backing or background fabric.

6. It is now ready for stitching and is then sewn on permanently. A variety of stitches can be chosen to stitch with, a common one being the satin stitch, which is very close zigzag stitches.

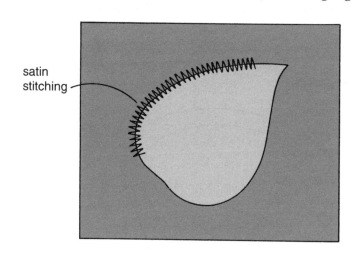

satin
stitching

Method 2

1. Draw or trace the mirror image of the appliqué shape onto tear–away stabilizer.

2. Pin or baste this shape to the wrong side of the backing or background fabric.

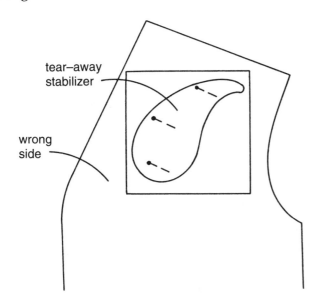

tear–away stabilizer

wrong side

3. Cut a square of appliqué fabric large enough to cover the desired appliqué shape.

4. Pin the wrong side of appliqué fabric to right side of background fabric covering the shape.

5. Set machine for normal straight stitch sewing and sew *completely around the design* from the underside.

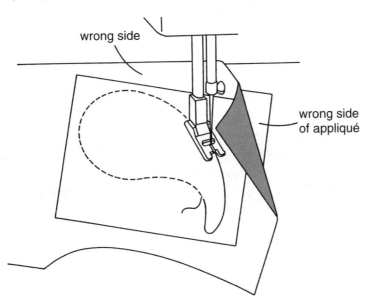

wrong side

wrong side of appliqué

Pro Quote

High–quality threads are often spun of longer fiber lengths, have less thread "fuzz," and generally break less often.

32

6. When stitching is completed turn to right side and with small, sharp embroidery scissors trim excess appliqué fabric away close to shape and stitched line. You may then want to satin stitch around the exterior of the design.

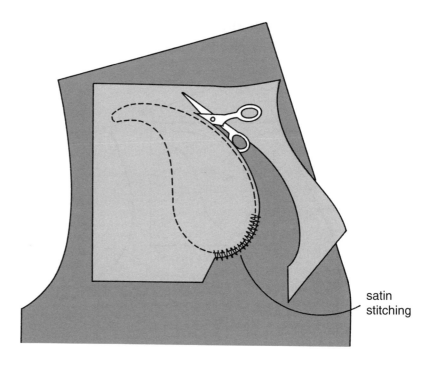

satin stitching

This sueded silk blouse is artfully embellished with complementary scrunched fabrics. They have been appliquéd on to a loose-hanging yoke. For more complete garment instructions, see the Project Page at the end of Chapter 7.

Stitching the Appliqué

- **The Stitch**—Since the edge of most appliqué motifs is a raw edge, it usually requires a close satin-type stitch to attach the shape to the backing or background fabric so that the raw edge is completely covered leaving no exposed fibers. A close zigzag stitch is referred to as a satin stitch. Other machine decorative satin stitch patterns can also be used.

Generally, set the machine for a very short stitch length which packs the zigzag close together. The wider you set your stitch width, the wider the satin stitch will be. Even though satin stitching can be done as wide as your machine will stitch, the wider the stitch, the more fabric will be pulled up between the stitches making an unwanted fabric tunnel. To help prevent this tunneling, use one of the following suggested methods to stabilize the fabric. The width of the satin stitch should be between 2.5 and 3.5 mm. Generally the larger the appliqué shape, the wider the satin stitch; the smaller the shape, the narrower the stitch.

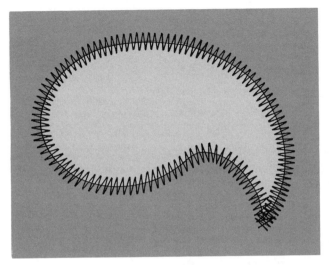 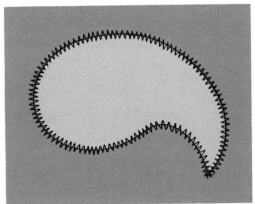

- **The Thread Tension**—Reduce the upper thread tension so that the bobbin thread will not pull up and show on the top side. Make sure to test sew a sample to achieve the desired result. Remember the sample must be the same composition as the article you are going to sew.

- **The Presser Foot**—Use an appliqué or open-toed presser foot, which has a large groove on the underside. This groove provides space under the foot for the satin stitches to flow freely, which then allows the fabric to flow evenly through the sewing machine.

groove

- **The Needle**—Generally, the heavier the fabric, the bigger the needle. When satin stitching on finer, lightweight fabrics use a 9/10 (70). Also use this size for single thicknesses of fabric. When you are working with heavier fabrics, especially in two or more layers, use a 12 (80) or 14 (90) needle.

When using metallic or rayon thread on the machine use a metalfil or new large-eyed embroidery needle. This metalfil needle helps to prevent thread breakage which is a common occurrence when using metallic threads.

- **The Thread**—High-quality, brand name threads work best when used for satin stitching. Less expensive, off brand threads are often spun from shorter fiber lengths which then will break more easily during the stitching process. High quality means that the thread has less "fuzz" on the thread, it will not break as often, and generally can produce a more lustrous finish. Try experimenting with different threads, especially extra–fine thread, threads designed especially for machine embroidery like rayon threads, and all the marvelous metallic threads. I have found that buying brand name metallic thread, using the metalfil needle, and sewing at a slower speed really pays off if you don't want to fight with breaking thread all the time.

Stabilizers

Whichever way you decide to appliqué the shape onto the backing or background fabric, the area to be stitched must be stabilized in some manner. This prevents puckering of the fabric during the stitching process.

Optional Stabilizing Choices

- Tear-away stabilizer can be pinned to the backing or background fabric or it can be held in place behind the fabric as the appliqué is stitched in place. Once the stitching is completed, the stabilizer is torn away. All that remains is the little bit that was caught in the actual stitching.

- Applying iron–on interfacing is also an option. This technique not only stabilizes the backing or background fabric, but also stiffens it. This stiffening effect must be considered in the final outcome because it will not be removed in the final garment or project. This is ideal for wall hangings, bags, belts, etc.

Large abstract motifs and shapes are appliquéd onto this polyester blouse following the instructions in Method 1 described in this chapter. For more complete details see Chapter 4's Project Page.

PRO QUOTE

To prevent fabric puckering when applying appliqué, choose an appropriate fabric stabilizer.

- Sandwiching the fabric in an embroidery hoop is a stabilizing method that allows the machine to stitch the fabric without it puckering. Then when the fabric is released from the hoop, the fabric is still relatively soft, maintaining its original suppleness (with the exception of the added stitching).

- Typewriter or computer paper can act as a paper stabilizer. It is put between the fabric and the throat plate. It sounds noisy when stitches go through it, but it tears away easily after sewing is completed.

The Satin–Stitch Technique

When stitching down your appliqué motif or shape, you may come across outside corners, inside corners, points, and curves. Here are some suggestions to assist in sewing these areas:

- **Outside Corners** — Satin stitch to the corner. Stop the machine with the needle down in the fabric on the *right hand side*. Pivot the fabric counter clock wise until it is lined up and ready to sew the next side. New stitches cover the previous stitches on the first edge.

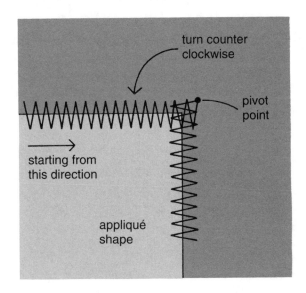

stop on right
pivot counter clockwise

• **Inside Corners** — Machine stitch past the corner to a distance equal to the width of the stitch. Stop the machine with the needle in the fabric on the *left hand side*. Pivot fabric clockwise until it is lined up and ready to sew the next edge. New stitches cover the previous stitches at the corner.

stop w/needle on left side
pivot clockwise

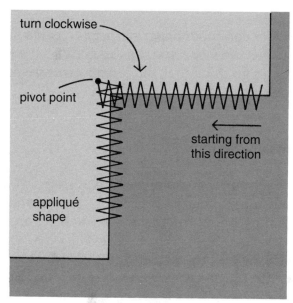

• **Points**—For very sharp points, begin tapering the satin stitch by narrowing the stitch width gradually to 0 as you get closer to the corner's point. The speed of the machine should be kept constant during this tapering process. Stop the machine with the needle in the point and pivot the work until you are headed down the other side. Then, when you start sewing again, begin gradually increasing the stitch width.

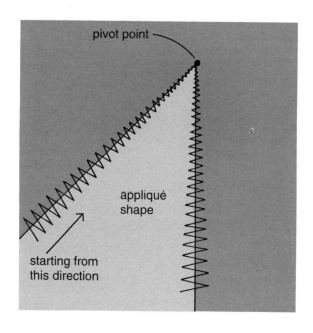

- **Curves**—For tight curves, stop the machine every few stitches and leave the needle in the fabric on the outside of the curve. Stitch and pivot the fabric slightly until you have completed the tight section. You will need to stop and pivot more frequently on a tighter curve.

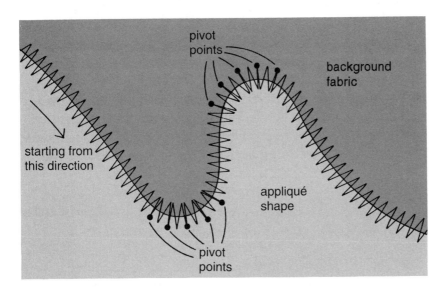

As always, if this is a first time experience for you, please take time to do some test samples. I have briefly touched on some of the basics of appliqué in this chapter. There are complete books dedicated to this subject. See the Resource List for further references if this is a subject of interest to you.

The Project Page

Appliqué Blouse

Appliqué: The Basics

Margaret Lawtie's lilac and grey blouse features free–flowing abstract appliqué shapes. A sampling of the shapes are identified and given to you. You can enlarge each of them to complement a full–sized adult pattern.

The blouse fabric is a solid-colored polyester microfiber. The appliqué shapes are cut in a complementary patterned fabric. A random design is cut out of the interior of the appliqué shape. The resulting hole is either filled with straight stitches using silver metallic thread, or it is filled with a pleated or scrunched fabric to highlight the hole. The appliqué shape has been applied using Method 1 (described in this chapter). The exterior and interior edges are satin stitched with silver metallic thread.

Further embellishment, in the form of sequins, beads, and bugle beads, are stitched on by hand to the areas indicated.

To visually connect all the shapes together, a braided cord is randomly couched to the surface. Sometimes the cord wanders over the appliqué shapes, and other times it is placed around the shape.

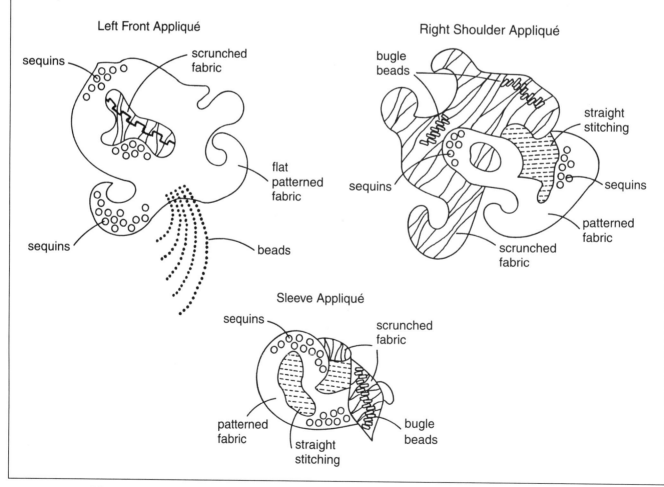

CHAPTER FIVE

FUN WITH FREEHAND EMBROIDERY

FREEHAND EMBROIDERY is also referred to as free–motion stitching. It opens up an entirely new world of creative stitching possibilities that you cannot do with the controlled stitch patterns your machine may offer.

You become the director of your machine as you guide the fabric in the directions and patterns you want. You are not restricted by the action of the feed dog.

SUGGESTED
APPLICATION
AND USAGE

Freehand embroidery can be used to outline or "sketch–stitch" designs onto the background fabric. You can also fill–in and create solidly stitched shapes. These techniques are also used in stitching monograms. Even though many current day computer sewing machines have built–in monogram letters, they may not be the same size or style that you would like to stitch, which makes freehand stitching your own monograms a viable option.

Some of the techniques explained in this book employ freehand embroidery techniques. As an example, see Chapter 11 on Fabriqué™ Mélange. Even though controlled, freehand stitching does require practice, the basic steps are very easy to achieve.

SPECIFIC
MATERIALS
AND SUPPLIES

- Darning foot
- Good quality embroidery thread
- Metalfil or embroidery needles
- Fabric
- Embroidery hoop
- Spring darning needle (optional)
- Flat bed for sewing machine

METHOD

Preparing Your Machine

You do not need a top–of–the–line computer sewing machine to freehand embroider. If your machine will zigzag as well as straight stitch, you can free-hand sew. You'll be able to create many alternative stitch designs and patterns. Once you learn the technique, you'll be the master of new stitch design creations.

1.   Attach the darning foot to your machine. You can freehand stitch without the darning foot; however, the foot helps to prevent skipped stitches, broken thread, broken needles, and (heaven forbid!) stitching through one's fingers. It holds the fabric against the throat plate while the stitch is being

PRO QUOTE

Freehand embroidery is often referred to as "fabric painting," because stitching by machine without the feed engaged allows you to stitch in any direction you want.

formed. Read your sewing machine's instruction manual to find the steps you need to take for darning and attaching the darning foot.

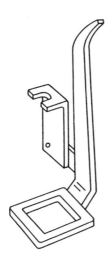

Alternatively, try using a spring darning needle on your machine rather than using the darning foot. Because the spring darning needle is sold with a universal 12/80 needle, it is advisable to change it to a metalfil needle — particularly when sewing with metallic and rayon threads.

Jenny's blue douppioni silk jacket features a myriad of Fabriqué™ techniques. The close-up of the shoulder detail illustrates how a simple piece of appliqué can create stunning emphasis by employing freehand stitching as the technique used to stitch the appliqué to the background fabric.

2. Use a top thread color to blend with the fabric or use a contrasting color. Your choice depends on the desired finished appearance. High-quality machine embroidery thread is recommended. Cotton, rayon, and metallic threads are optional choices. Your practice sessions can be done in cotton thread; however, be aware that cotton thread will more easily shred and break. When you go on to your final project, try using rayon and metallic threads, which will add luster, sheen, and special effects to the final design.

3. Bobbin thread can be of matching or contrasting color and texture. Some machines will operate best if the same texture of thread is in the bobbin. If your machine functions well when using different top and bobbin threads, cotton basting thread or monofilament nylon bobbin fill can be used in the bobbin.

4. Upper thread tension is usually decreased two to three numbers lower. When stitching, you do not want the bobbin thread to pull to the top side — particularly if you are using a contrasting color in the bobbin. Therefore, experiment on your practice samples to get your machine tension suitable for your choice of thread and fabric.

5. Lower or cover the feed dog. All machines are somewhat different in how the feed dog is lowered or covered. Refer to the machine's instruction manual in the section on darning and/or freehand embroidery for the specific procedures to use with your machine. Alternatively, check with your sewing machine dealer. You need to lower or cover the feed dog so its fabric feed–through action will not interfere with your control and directing the fabric movement.

6. Machine needles must always be sharp and new. If they are dull, bent, or slightly damaged, they can cause grief in skipped stitches and thread breakage. Metalfil or new embroidery needles are recommended for all freehand embroidery.

Preparing Your Fabric

Fabric must be stabilized in a hoop to prevent the fabric from puckering up on itself, the stitches from skipping, and the thread from breaking. When the fabric is in the hoop, hold the hoop down on the table and gently pull on the fabric all the way

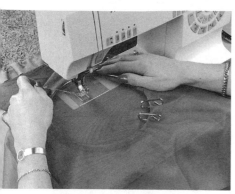

Fabric is stretched "tight as a drum" inside the embroidery hoop. With the first stitch, the bobbin thread should always be pulled up to the top of the fabric to prevent being caught in the subsequent stitching.

around the hoop. The fabric should be taut without having any folds or puckers, and you must be careful not to distort the fabric grainline. After the fabric is placed and tightened in the hoop, the fabric should end up being as "tight as a drum."

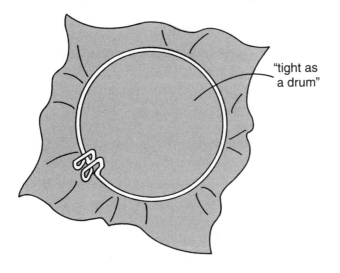

"tight as a drum"

Stitching Technique

1. Begin by placing the fabric in the hoop. Set machine for straight stitch. Lower the presser foot. If your machine has a half–way presser-tension position, lower to this position. If not, lower the presser foot the total amount.

2. Take one stitch. Pull the bobbin thread up to the right side. Then securely hold on to both the upper and lower threads when you begin stitching.

PRO QUOTE

To freehand embroider, fabric must be placed in an embroidery hoop and it must be stretched as "tight as a drum."

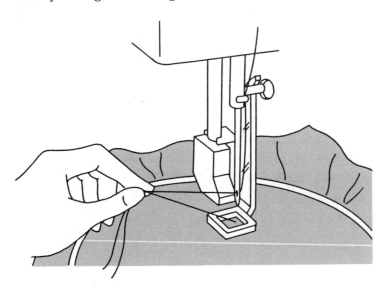

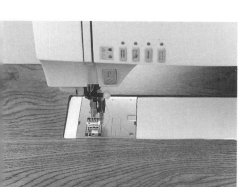

When freehand stitching, it is much easier to control the direction of the hoop and fabric if the sewing machine bed is surrounded by a flat surface that is level with the bed of the machine. A good example of a flat bed insert is shown here.

PRO QUOTE

Freehand embroidering is much easier to do if you create or insert a flat bed table at the same level and surround the bed of the sewing machine.

This prevents the bobbin thread from being sewn into the other stitches of the work, which would make an untidy finish. When you begin stitching, take several stitches in the same spot to secure the threads. When stitching is completed, trim threads.

3. Create a flatbed around the throat plate of your machine. This offers a stable area for the hoop and fabric. If you are fortunate enough to have a sewing machine cabinet with an air lift platform, position it in the flatbed level and surround your machine with a shaped flatbed insert. Alternatively, have a handyman make a wooden template cut to surround the shape of your machine. You could also create a temporary flatbed with a stack of thick books placed to the left of the needle plate. Also, some machines have attachable extension tables.

4. Once you begin stitching, it may at first seem awkward without the feed dog moving the fabric. This process is most easily done if you follow these guidelines. Sit comfortably with your elbows on the table and relax. Hold the hoop with your fingers. Move the hoop with a gentle, fluid, and caressing action. Do not move the hoop in rapid, jerky motions. Direct the hoop where you want to do the stitching. Run the machine fairly fast and move the hoop with even hand and wrist motions. If the machine runs slow and you move the hoop fast, you create longer, generally uneven stitches.

Make sure you do some practice samples before beginning on the final fabric. It is helpful to take a piece of test muslin or cotton and mark it with a grid pattern as shown. Secure this in the hoop. Within each grid, stitch in the pattern as indicated.

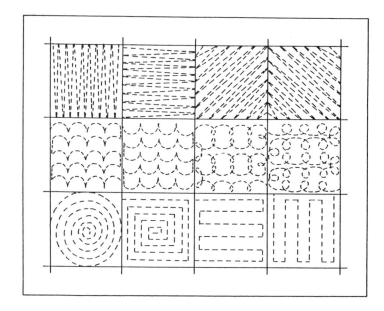

Also practice writing your name until you are comfortable with the procedure and outcome.

You might also like to try freehand stitching with a zigzag stitch approximately 3mm wide. It creates a totally different effect than stitching with a straight stitch. Set the stitch pattern for zigzag. Stitch in various directions. Generally, moving the hoop from east to west (side to side), you will be able to color or fill in a design. If you move the hoop from north to south (back and forth), the stitch forms a satin stitch. Once again, practice writing your name with freehand zig-zag stitching and observe the difference than when writing with straight stitching.

Remember that in the introduction to this book I mentioned patience. If you've never done freehand embroidery before, it is easy to do once you get the hang of it. Take a day when not too much else is happening for you. Put some relaxing music on, make yourself a cup of tea, and just begin sewing. Set up a test sample of fabric with the grid pattern (as illustrated above) and stitch in all directions indicated. Do this grid stitching as many times as you need to in order to get the hang of it. The more practice you do, the more comfortable it will feel. Relax, have patience, and enjoy this learning process — the rewards will be significant when you can stitch without the directional control of the feed dog.

- If the bobbin thread shows:

  — Decrease the top thread tension. You may want to have the same color thread on the bobbin as well as the top so that they match, or use a clear, monofilament bobbin fill.

- If the top thread breaks or shreds:

  — Top tension may be too tight.

  — Try tightening the fabric in the hoop, remember it needs to be very tight, "tight as a drum."

PRO QUOTE

When learning to freehand stitch, allow yourself at least ten hours of practice time to feel comfortable with the technique.

TROUBLE SHOOTING

— You may have stitched over the same area too much, therefore try to maintain a more even flow when moving the hoop.

— The needle may be dull.

— Eye of the needle is too small. Change to a needle with a larger eye.

— Thread could be of poor quality.

— With fast sewing, the top thread may have spun off the spool and onto the spindle. Try covering the spool with a spool cover or cotton finger bandage.

— Metallic threads shred and break easily. Use a metalfil needle.

— You may have been pressing on the speed control unevenly. Run machine at even medium to fast speed.

• Bobbin thread breaks:

— Clean the bobbin case.

— The bobbin thread may have come out of the tension gauge because you are "speeding" with the machine. Check and rethread.

— Try loosening the bobbin tension.

— Make sure the bobbin is evenly wound.

• Threads may seem to tangle and jam up quite rapidly:

— Check to make sure you have *lowered your presser foot*. This can be easily overlooked with freehand embroidery.

— Check to make sure both top and bobbin threads are in their respective thread guides.

• The needle breaks:

— It may be the wrong size for the fabric and thread you are using. Very fine needles break more easily. Generally a standard 12/80 or 14/90 are satisfactory.

PRO QUOTE

Always move the hoop with a gentle, fluid, caressing hand action when freehand embroidery stitching.

— You may be moving the hoop too fast and jerky. Or you could be doing the reverse, sewing too slowly, which will cause the fabric to drag on the needle. Practice with steady yet fast speed and even hoop movement.

— The area being stitched is very bulky or dense. If you can, rearrange the fabric layers. Leave the dense area till last and be as careful as possible.

— The machine foot may loosen with constant, fast stitching. Check and retighten needle clamp screw.

Mastering the skills of freehand embroidery opens up many avenues for self-expression. In this accessories group, the handbag, constructed of black satin, features repetitive freehand stitching done with gold metallic thread. The eyeglasses case and belt buckle also use freehand stitching to enhance their final embellishment.

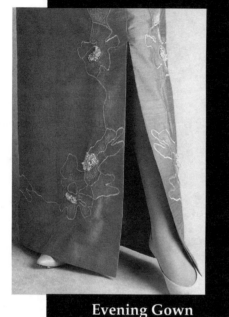

Fun with Freehand Embroidery

The project featured in this chapter is the mauve evening gown in douppioni silk from Margaret. The area to be embellished is the hem line and walking slit.

Machine satin stitching with gold metallic thread forms the major outline of the design. Using a disappearing fabric-marking pen, transfer the shapes to be satin stitched onto the right side of the fabric. Enclosed spaces are created as the stitching progresses. Straight lines of freehand embroidery, stitched with gold metallic thread, fill some of the spaces as indicated. Other spaces are filled with hand stitching on clusters of seed pearls and gold beads.

These stitch patterns and shapes are repeated in a mirror image on the left hand side of the hem line and walking slit. On the back of the garment at the hem line, a repetition of these basic forms can be drawn and stitched.

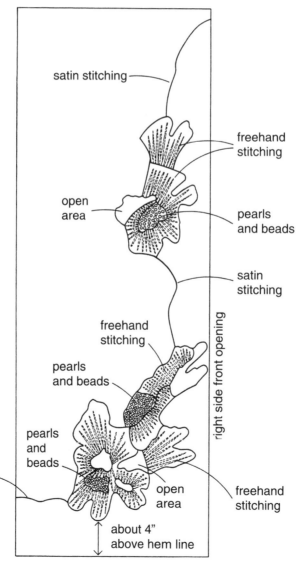

This elegant Fabriqué™ evening gown is one of Margaret Lawtie's creations. It has been artfully embellished with freehand embroidery. You will find this more fully explained in Chapter 5's Project Page. Below is shown a detailed close-up of a section of the hemline.

Glenda's fuchsia-gold-black vest shows a multitude of Fabriqué™ processes. This vest is featured as a completely detailed project in Chapter 15.

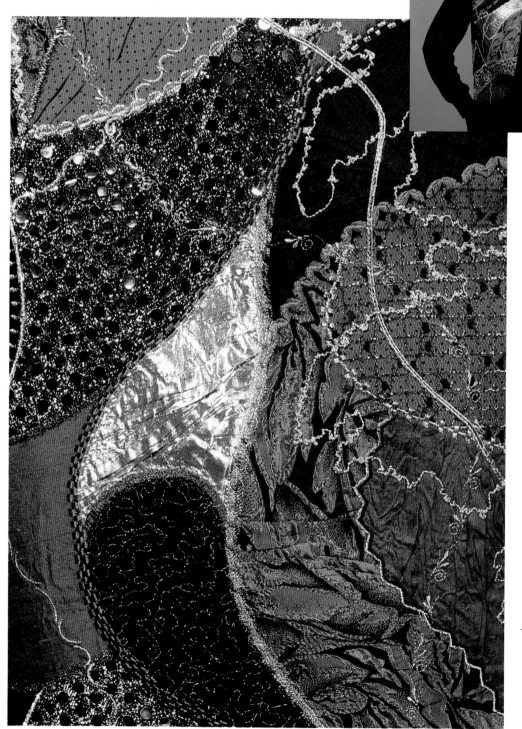

Note some of the creative details on the back of this vest. Decorative machine stitching using gold metallic thread, couching and dribbling are some of the techniques used for embellishing this garment.

Similar Fabriqué™ techniques were incorporated on these stunning vests. Chapter 15 gives you guidelines for designing the appliqué shapes — either free-flowing or abstract geometrics.

This creative work by Jenny Anastas maximizes the use of many decorative stitch patterns on the sewing machine.

Jenny Anastas created this Woven Magic fabric panel which has been used as the front of this vest. You too can weave magic into your projects. See Chapter 9.

Woven Magic blouse from Jenny. Note the cable stitching details which further enhance both front and back yoke. Jenny completed this spectacular ensemble when she made the complementary woven magic handbag. Details for stitching this handbag are found in Chapter 9's Project Page.

Margaret Lawtie's green silk jacket illustrates the Fabriqué™ technique of designing with torn strips. See Chapter 8. On the other hand, her green silk vest features the Fabriqué™ scrunching method 4 found in Chapter 7. The detailed insert gives you an enlargement of this innovative technique.

Glenda's Tubes 'n Tunnels technique is shown embellishing the beautiful raw silk jacket. Chapter 13 gives you all the details for this easy process.

This brown wool vest illustrates asymmetrical balance. The Fabriqué™ techniques of scrunching, torn strip applications, and tubes 'n tunnels are the main techniques shown here.

This dramatic red silk jacket illustrates the use of
couching, cable stitching, and straight stitching.
Margaret's easy-to-do jacket is featured in the Project
Page of Chapter 12.

CHAPTER SIX

PUCKERING WITH SCRIBBLE STITCHES

Puckering is a form of freehand embroidery, *without* using an embroidery hoop. The fabric is pulled in, puckered up, and molded as you scribble stitch. This process in itself creates a three-dimensional surface. Puckering is a truly easy, no mistake type of fabric manipulation. Simply follow these easy steps and guidelines.

50

Suggested Application and Usage

Once the fabric is puckered, if you want to use it as part of your embellished garment, bond the wrong side with paper–backed fusible webbing, cut the desired pattern shape, and peel back the paper backing from the fusible webbing. You are now ready to apply this puckered fabric onto the backing or background fabric.

Further to this fabric-puckering technique, you can now add decorative machine stitches, beadwork, couched yarns, braids, or heavy threads on the top surface.

Puckered fabric can be cut into any pattern shape. Depending on the quantity of fabric you pucker, you could cut yokes, cuffs, or collars. Or, you can cut irregular and unique shapes and use it to create contrast and embellishment on any jacket, vest, or blouse pattern. This technique was used as one of the appliqué shapes on the fuchsia–black–gold vest featured in Chapter 15.

Specific Materials and Supplies

• Paper–backed fusible webbing
• Soft, drapable fabric
• Thread
• Darning foot or spring darning needle
• Color compatible or contrasting embroidery thread

Method

1. Machine is set for straight stitching.

2. Use regular thread tension. Tensions can also be increased or decreased, which will change the final effect of the stitching on the fabric.

3. Use either a contrasting color of rayon, metallic or cotton–polyester thread, or use thread that blends in color with the fabric to be puckered.

4. Use a darning foot or spring darning needle on the machine. Make sure the accompanying needle is new.

5. Any fabric that is light to medium weight and is drapable can be puckered. For example: chiffon, lightweight satin, silky polyester, polyester microfibers, or soft, drapy silks.

Pro Quote

Change to a metalfil needle in the spring darning needle especially when working with metallic and rayon threads.

6. Because this employs freehand stitching, the feed dog is down or covered, and not engaged.

7. Begin stitching fabric that has *not* been secured in a hoop. As you stitch, leave at least 1" (2.5 cm) of fabric at the edges so that you will have some fabric to hold on to as you stitch close to the edge. As the machine takes stitch after stitch, the fabric will automatically pull up and bubble or pucker into itself.

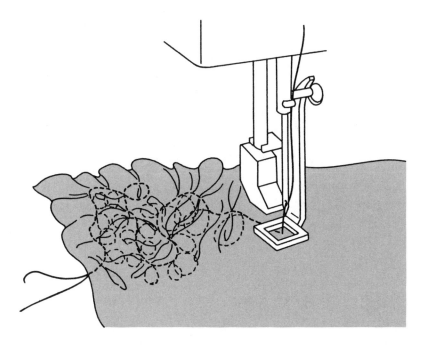

8. Stitching should be in circles, semi–circle shell formations, or you can wander the stitches in a cornelly type of design. See Chapter 2 on Know the Terms. Think of this as scribbling with stitches on top of the fabric. The closer you keep the stitches, the tighter the bubbles and puckers will be. Occasionally, the fabric may get pulled down into the throat

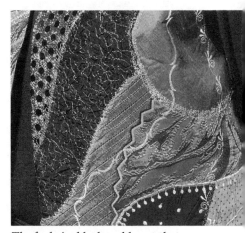

The fuchsia–black–gold vest that is fully explained in Chapter 15, features three puckered appliqué shapes. The process of puckering with scribble stitches texturizes the fabric's surface prior to it being appliquéd to the backing fabric.

plate. Stop stitching immediately and pull the fabric back up. Keep a slow, even, and consistent speed when running the machine. Use both hands to guide the fabric while stitching.

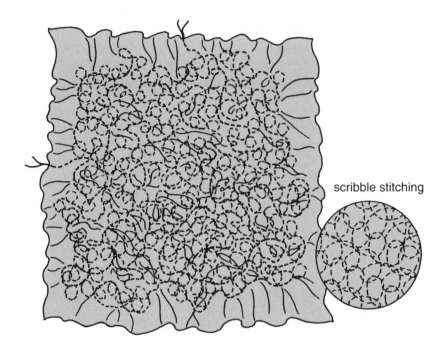

scribble stitching

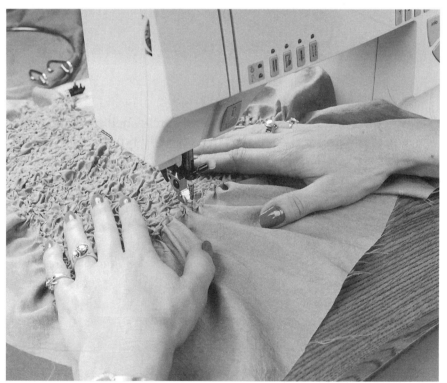

A very lightweight, drapable polyester is being "puckered." Puckering is a form of freehand stitching that does not require the fabric to be stretched in a hoop. The machine's feed dog is lowered or covered.

Puckering with Scribble Stitches

This fabric-puckering project is quick and easy to do. Decide on the blouse fabric and the colors of fabric that will look good appliquéd onto it. I choose a sturdy blue polyester for the blouse, a multicolored chiffon in blues, greens, and burgundy colors, and a solid burgundy colored, shimmering chiffon. Use any simple shirt or blouse pattern without shoulder yokes. Cut out all pattern pieces. Do not proceed with pattern construction until all appliqué work is completed.

Pucker both chiffons with *scribble stitching* as described in this chapter. I used gold metallic thread to complement the multicolored chiffon that was already shot with gold.

Draw the appliqué shapes on paper-backed, fusible webbing. Cut out these shapes. Bond the fusible web to the wrong side of the puckered fabric. Remove the paper backing and then bond the puckered appliqué shape onto the blouse in locations indicated.

Stitch appliqué shapes to background fabric using a regular satin stitch, a decorative satin stitch pattern, or a cornelly-type stitch. Remember to stabilize the area to be stitched by using a tear–away stabilizer or by securing the fabric in a hoop before stitching. Add any other decorative stitch patterns running through and beyond the appliquéd shapes. Now you are ready to complete the garment construction steps according to the instruction guide sheet.

Puckered Appliqué

embroidery motif

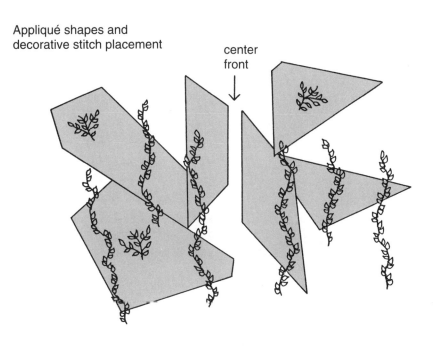

Appliqué shapes and decorative stitch placement

center front

wandering decorative stitch pattern

Personal Notes

CHAPTER SEVEN

SCRUNCHING FOR TEXTURE

S CRUNCHING is one of the most exciting yet simple fabric-manipulation techniques. Four methods will be described. All are easy and all create a slightly different outcome. Most fabrics can be manually scrunched; however, fabrics that don't crease easily, like some polyesters, lend themselves best to Method 2 and 3, which use gathering stitches.

SUGGESTED APPLICATION AND USAGE

Scrunched fabric can be used in a variety of ways. Depending on the scrunching technique you use, many applications are possible.

Method 1 hand twists the fabric, which can be cut into appliqué shapes and then incorporated as part of an entire design.

Method 2 and 3 both use gathering stitches. In Method 2, you gather the fabric after the stitching is done. In Method 3, elastic thread is wound on the bobbin which begins the texturizing process as the stitching is being done.

Method 4, which pushes the fabric under the presser foot with a knitting needle or wooden skewer, is great when used as a surface embellishment. See the green vest on color plate #6.

All methods produce significantly different results. They can all be used as appliqué shapes or additionally, an entire pattern piece — such as a yoke, cuff, or pocket — could be cut and sewn into the garment.

SPECIFIC MATERIALS AND SUPPLIES

- Fabric
- Thread
- Elastic thread
- Paper–backed fusible webbing
- Knitting needle or wooden skewer
- Rubber bands
- Appliqué mat
- Tracing vellum
- Disappearing fabric-marking pen
- Embroidery hoop or tear–away stabilizer

METHOD 1

Scrunching by Hand Twisting The Fabric

Fabrics could be silk, lamé, rayon, taffeta, lightweight cottons, or any fabric that holds wrinkles well.

1. Using the piece of fabric that is to be scrunched, take hold of each side. With each side, form finger pinch pleats and hold securely.

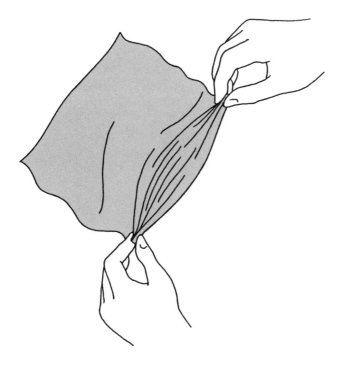

2. Begin twisting the pinch-pleated fabric. Keep twisting until the fabric starts to curl up onto itself and forms a bunchy, little knot.

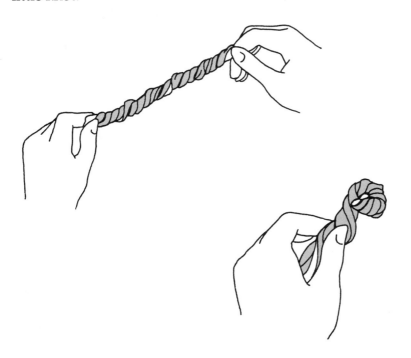

3. Using a steam iron, press down hard on both sides of the rolled and twisted fabric. Delicate, heat-sensitive fabrics may need to be protected with a press cloth.

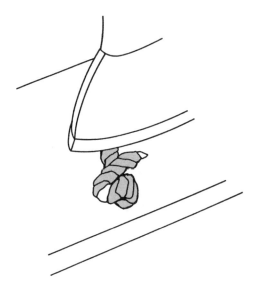

4. Wrap rubber bands around the twisted, curled fabric and let it cool. The longer you let it sit at this stage, the more scrunched the fabric will be.

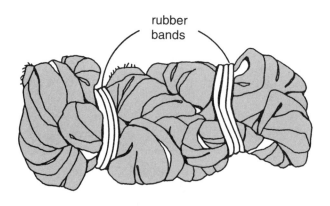

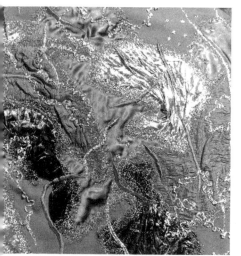

When creating with abstract shapes and motifs, let your imagination be totally adventuresome. Scrunching by hand twisting the fabric (Method 1 in this chapter) was the process used to texturize the appliqué fabric before it was cut into geometric, abstract shapes and appliquéd to the yoke of this blouse.

5. Release the rubber bands and untwist the fabric. Smooth the fabric a little bit leaving scrunched, raised sections. It is up to you how much you open up and smooth the fabric.

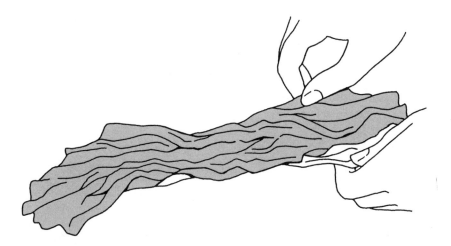

6. On the ironing board, place paper–backed, fusible webbing with the fusible side face up. Lay the scrunched fabric wrong side down. Place appliqué mat, a piece of tracing vellum, or a piece of baking parchment over top. Gently press to adhere fusible webbing to the scrunched fabric.

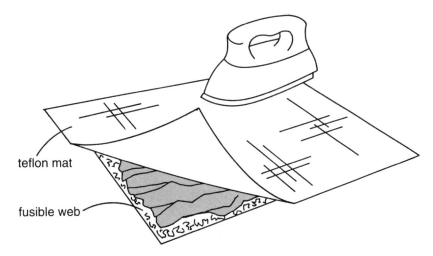

teflon mat

fusible web

7. Cut to desired shape, remove paper backing from fusible web, and bond to the backing or background fabric. To complete the application, satin stitch (or use a decorative stitch pattern) to secure the appliqué to the fabric.

METHOD 2

Scrunching with Gathering Stitches

1. Using the fabric to be scrunched, run long, gathering stitches horizontally, diagonally, or vertically along the fabric. The rows of stitches can be close together ($\frac{1}{4}$" [.6 cm]) or further apart ($\frac{1}{2} - \frac{3}{4}$" [1.3–1.9 cm]) depending on the tightness of the scrunch. The rows of stitching can be parallel to each other, or they can wobble from narrow to wide width. Inconsistency in spacing will simply give a different look.

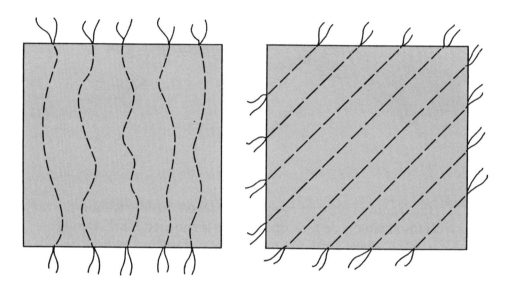

The thread used will influence the outcome. Thread of the same color will blend with the final, scrunched fabric. A contrasting gold or silver thread will give highlights to the final surface texture.

2. Pull the gathering stitches up as tight as you wish, thereby creating a puffy, rumpled, and bumpled look.

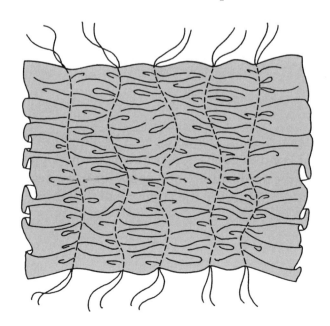

PRO QUOTE

When fabric does not hold sharp creases, try scrunching with gathering stitches using either regular thread or elastic thread in the bobbin.

3. On your ironing board, place the paper–backed fusible webbing with paper side down and fusible side up. Place wrong side of scrunched and gathered fabric on top of the paper–backed fusible.

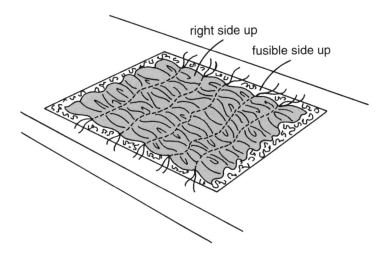

4. Work and manipulate the gathers until the desired rumpled look is achieved. Then place an appliqué mat or a piece of tracing vellum on top. Press to adhere fusible webbing to wrong side of scrunched fabric.

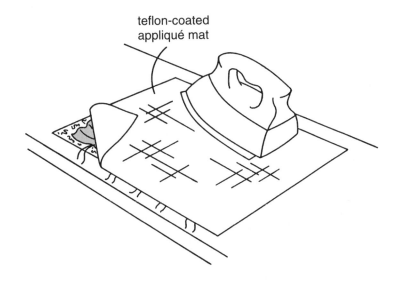

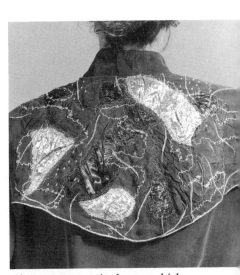

Abstract geometric shapes, which were initially scrunched by hand twisting to create surface texture, have been artfully appliquéd to the back yoke of this blouse. Creative credit goes to Jenny Anastas.

5. Let the fabric cool. The gathering stitches will not be removed. No matter whether you've used thread of a complementary or contrasting color, or metallic thread, the stitches will remain as an integral part of the design.

6. The pattern piece or appliqué shape should then be cut to the desired size. After removing the paper backing it can be bonded in place to the backing or background fabric. To complete the application, satin stitch (or use a decorative stitch pattern) to secure the appliqué to the fabric.

METHOD 3

Scrunching using Elastic Thread

This particular technique works well on polyesters that ordinarily would not hold a crease well. It works fine on fabrics that are soft as well as those that have a high luster or sheen. It uses gathering stitches; however, elastic thread is wound on the bobbin.

1. Wind a bobbin, by hand, with elastic thread. Do not put much tension on the thread as you wind it on the bobbin.

2. Set the machine for a long, basting stitch length.

3. The upper thread can be a color of thread that matches or blends with the fabric — or it can be a contrasting gold or silver metallic or rayon thread. Remember to use a metalfil needle when using metallic or rayon thread.

4. Cut a piece of fabric at least 8" (20 cm) x 10" (25 cm).

5. With a disappearing fabric-marking pen, draw randomly curving stitching lines on the right side of the fabric.

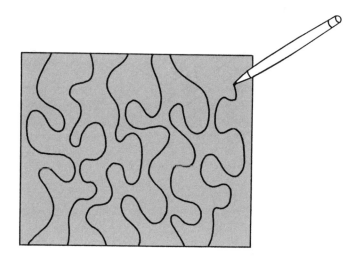

6. Begin the basting stitching, always starting and stopping each line of stitching on either side of the fabric. Since there is elastic thread in the bobbin, the fabric will automatically begin to pull up.

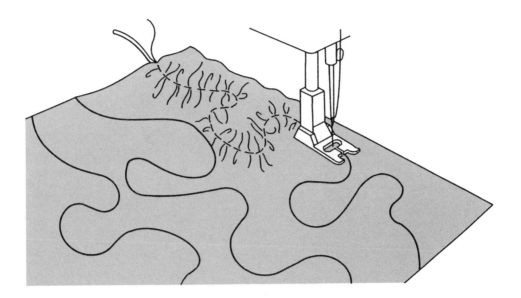

7. Pull up elastic bobbin thread, gathering stitches until you create the desired amount of puffiness.

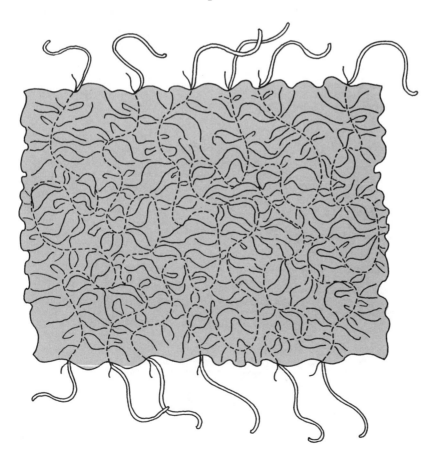

You can now treat this scrunched fabric in one of two ways.

Suggestion #1

1. Decide on an appliqué shape. Add $1/4''$ (.6 cm) to the outside edges. Cut scrunched fabric by this shape.

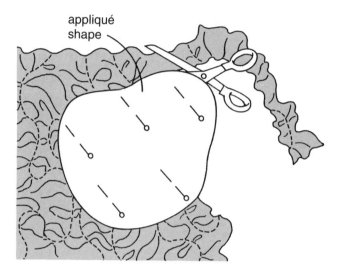

appliqué shape

2. Pin appliqué shape to backing or background fabric.

3. Straight stitch around appliqué shape. Make sure that backing or background fabric has been stabilized by inserting in embroidery hoop or by backing with tear–away stabilizer.

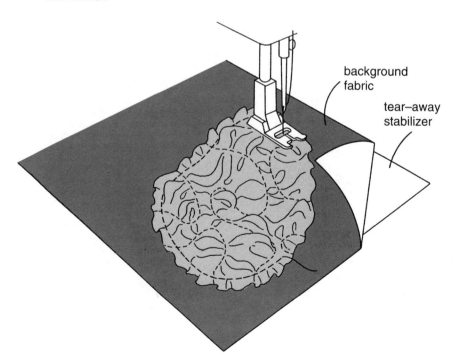

background fabric

tear–away stabilizer

4. Trim raw edges of appliqué shape close to stitching line. Stitch over top of straight stitching with a satin stitch (or decorative satin stitch) thereby enclosing the raw edge and the line of straight stitching.

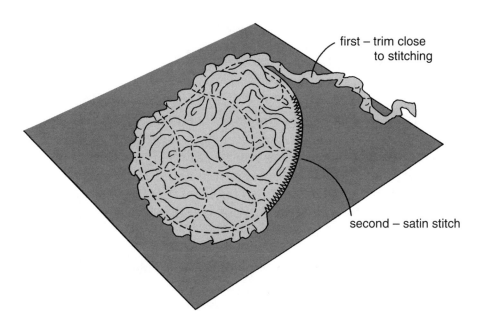

first – trim close to stitching

second – satin stitch

Suggestion #2

1. On your ironing board, place paper–backed fusible webbing with paper side down and fusible side up. Place wrong side of scrunched and gathered fabric on top of paper–backed fusible webbing. Place appliqué mat or a piece of tracing vellum on top of fabric.

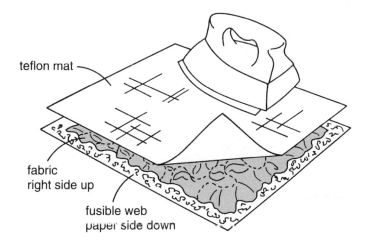

teflon mat

fabric right side up

fusible web paper side down

2. Press to adhere fusible webbing to wrong side of scrunched fabric.

3. The pattern piece or appliqué shape is then cut to desired size. Remove paper backing and bond in place to the backing or background fabric. To complete the application, satin stitch (or use a decorative stitch pattern) to secure the appliqué to the fabric.

METHOD 4

Scrunching by Pushing Fabric under the Presser Foot

This technique is done by machine. It is a manipulation of the fabric by pushing it evenly or randomly under the presser foot with a knitting needle or wooden skewer while you continue sewing. This method generally is stitched directly onto the background fabric.

PRO QUOTE

Chinese chop sticks work wonderfully for scrunching fabric by pushing the fabric under the presser foot as you sew.

1. Set the machine for straight stitch. Use regular presser foot.

2. For a sample, take the fabric to be scrunched, about 12" (31 cm) long x 3" (8 cm) wide, and lay it on top of the background fabric. For more stability, place the background fabric securely in an embroidery hoop or back with tear–away stabilizer.

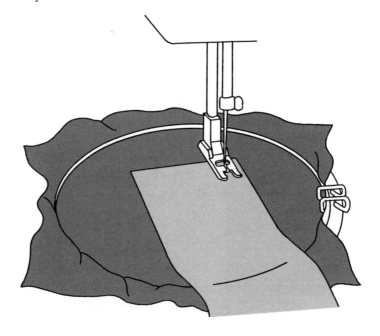

3. Begin stitching about $^1/_4$" (.6 cm) away from the raw edge of the fabric to be scrunched.

4. With the point of a knitting needle, embroidery scissors, or a wooden skewer, manually begin pushing the fabric underneath the presser foot as you are stitching.

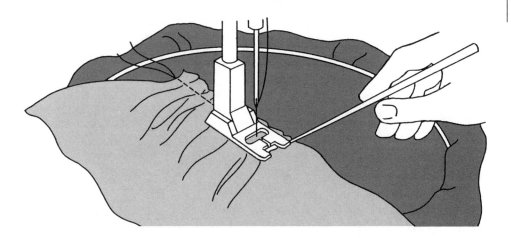

5. Repeat this fabric-pushing process until the length of the fabric has been scrunched. Sew around the corner and continue pushing the fabric under the presser foot. As you sew up the other side the little scrunches will be pushed under the presser foot in the opposite direction to the first side you just stitched. This adds textural variety to the scrunched fabric.

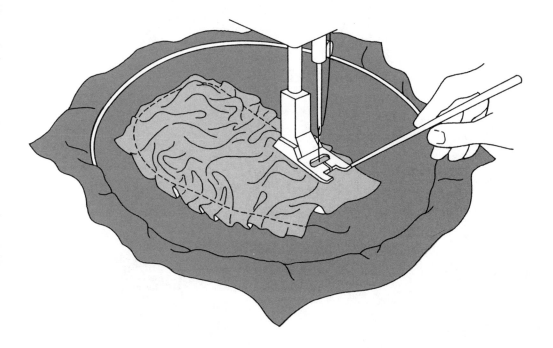

6. You will have created a three-dimensional bubble. Trim excess scrunched fabric next to the stitching line. Use a satin stitch (or a decorative satin stitch) to cover raw edges, thereby securing the fabric bubble to the background fabric.

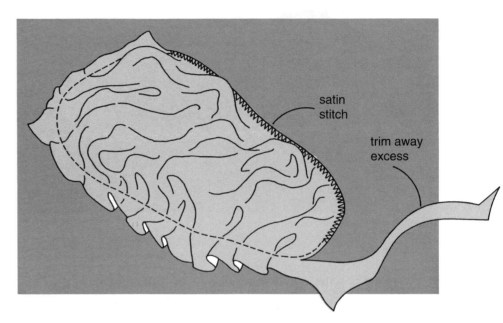

This silk vest was embellished by Margaret Lawtie. To get a really good look at one of the scrunched fabric groupings, take a look at this close-up. All scrunching was done by pushing the fabric under the presser foot with a wooden skewer while stitching it to the background fabric.

7. You may want the "bubble" to remain if it is used for a wall hanging or other unwearable item. However, if you plan on wearing the finished piece, the bubble will likely not stay "puffed" once it is washed; therefore, I recommend that you stitch one (if not more) row(s) of straight stitches (or any decorative satin stitches) down the center of the bubble. Use contrasting colored threads for a more outstanding appearance, or a thread color that blends for a tone–on–tone appearance. This, in itself, adds additional surface texture to the manipulated fabric.

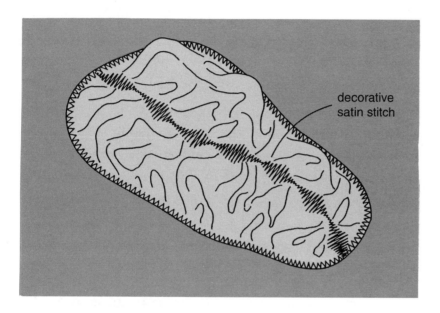

decorative
satin stitch

Scrunched Embellishment

Scrunching for Texture

If you liked our green silk blouse shown on color plate #13, scrunching by hand twisting the fabric is the dominant texturizing process used. Both front and back yokes are first embellished with scrunched appliquéd fabric and then the yokes are stitched in place over the entire bodice. The yokes are sewn into the neck, shoulder, and armscye seams. The yokes are lined to cover up all the wrong side stitching and the bottom edge of the yoke and lining were satin stitched together with gold metallic thread.

The green background fabric is sand–washed silk. This color plus black and burgundy-colored silk, gold lamé, and a black and gold brocade are the fabrics that were scrunched.

The fabrics are scrunched, and then they are appliquéd to the background fabric using Method 1 from Chapter 4 — Appliqué: The Basics. Each shape is stitched to the background fabric by either a cornelly-type stitch pattern or by using a freehand serpentine stitch.

Further embellishment was done using satin stitch bursts, which are stitched in gold metallic and burgundy-colored rayon threads. To do a satin stitch burst, set the machine for zigzag, and the stitch length at .3 to .35 mm. Set the stitch width at 0. With the machine running at an even speed, gradually increase the stitch width to 3 mm, stitch for a short distance, then gradually decrease the stitch width to 0 again.

Final embellishment is stitched over the top of the whole design using the technique of dribbling, as described in Chapter 12.

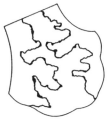

Location of dribbling
on Right Front Yoke

Location of bursts
on Right Front Yoke

0 mm width

3 mm width

0 mm width

Satin stitch burst

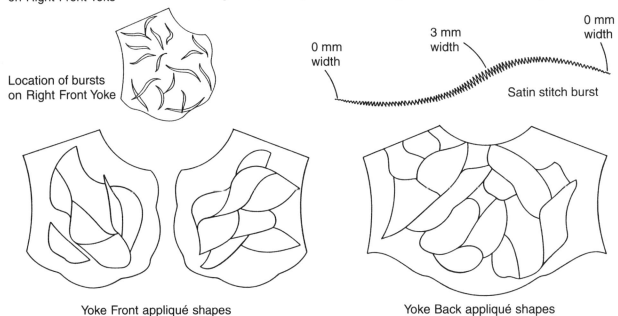

Yoke Front appliqué shapes

Yoke Back appliqué shapes

CHAPTER EIGHT

STUNNING FABRIC STRIPS

T HIS CHAPTER IS DEVOTED TO TAKING STRIPS OF FABRIC and manipulating them to create stunning and unique garment embellishment. Fabric strips can be randomly clustered or geometrically grouped. This simple process, creates an effective form of clothing embellishment.

SUGGESTED APPLICATION AND USAGE

You may want clusters of fabric strips grouped in random locations, or you may want straight lines of scrunched strips running the length or width of the pattern.

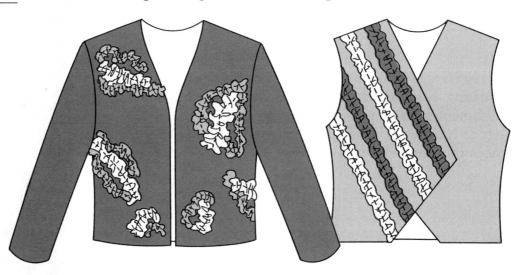

You might visually connect your cluster groups by dribbling (see Chapter 12 on Couching, Cable Stitching, and Dribbling), or stitching with a decorative machine stitch, randomly wandering from group to group.

PRO QUOTE

Clustering strips of fabric with contrasting textures like polyester satin, netting, lace, and brocade can produce an attractive composition on the fabric's surface.

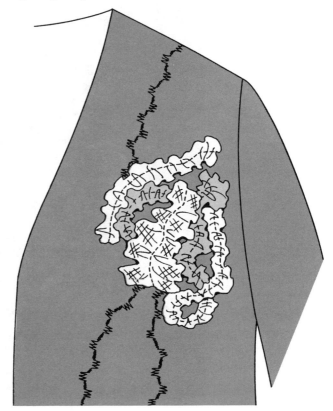

You may want to finish off a cluster grouping of fabric strips by sewing on some beads, bugles, or sequins.

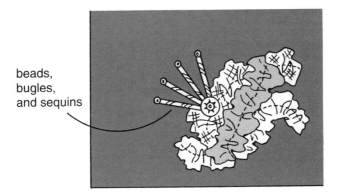

beads,
bugles,
and sequins

Various strips of fabric in different colors and textures can also be combined or woven together. See Chapter 9 on Woven Magic.

You might use store-purchased ribbons and laces to combine with your fabric strips. These laces and ribbons can also be scrunched or gathered prior to sewing them into the project.

The creative choice is up to you. Think about how you would like the final garment to look. Play around with the pattern and fabric. Pin clusters of strips in place to get a visual feel of the outcome. Remember, you can make no mistakes.

- Fabric
- Thread
- Knitting needle or wooden skewer
- Tear–away stabilizer
- Liquid stabilizer (optional)
- Ribbons and lace (optional)
- Beads, bugles, or sequins (optional)

Preparation of Fabric Strips

Either cut or tear strips of fabric. They can be as narrow as ¼″ (.6 cm) or as wide as 1″ to 1 ½″ (2.5–3.8 cm).

The following techniques are suggestions for treating and finishing the long edges of the fabric strips.

Torn strips of satin and glitzy tubes of gold lamé are randomly woven together to create Jenny's woven magic fabric. Once the fabric panel was woven, it was used to form the front of this vest.

SPECIFIC MATERIALS AND SUPPLIES

METHOD

• **Torn Edging** — The strips of fabric can be "torn," leaving the raw edge just slightly frayed-looking. When using this raw edge treatment, gentle care for the garment would be required so that additional fraying would not occur.

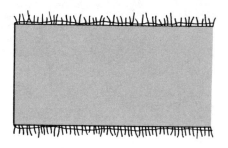

• **Fringed Edging** — On a wider fabric strip — 1" to 1 ½" (2.5 to 3.8 cm) straight stitch about ¼" (.6 cm) in from the long edge, or use a narrow zigzag stitch. Fringe the edge by pulling out all the fabric fibers that are parallel to the stitching, leaving the perpendicular fibers to form a fringed edge.

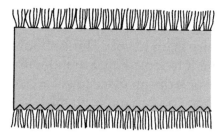

• **Rolled Hem Edging** — With the serger, sew a rolled hem edge on both sides of the fabric strip.

• **Decorative Satin Edging** — Sew the long edges of the fabric strips with a decorative satin stitch from your conventional sewing machine. You may want to turn the edge under ¼" (.6 cm) to the wrong side thereby creating a cleaner more stable edge to sew the decorative satin stitch onto. You may also want to initially stabilize the edge by placing a strip of "tear–away" fabric stabilizer under the edge or by using a liquid fabric stabilizer like Perfect Sew. (First, make sure you test the liquid fabric stabilizer on test fabric following the manufacturer's directions.)

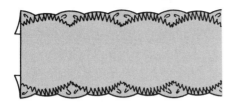

Application of Fabric Strips

- Take the prepared fabric strip and attach it to the garment fabric to be embellished. I recommend attaching it by following Scrunching Method 4 in Chapter 7. Set your sewing machine for straight stitching. Use a knitting needle or wooden skewer to push the fabric strip under the presser foot as you sew down the *center* of the fabric strip.

- Or, sew a row of basting stitches down the center length of the fabric strip. Gather as much as desired. Then place gathered strip onto fabric to be embellished in parallel rows or have strips meandering in any direction that you want. Stitch in place with either a straight stitch or a decorative embroidery stitch.

Strips of black satin, gold netting, and black and gold lace are stitched in cluster grouping on Margaret's green silk jacket.

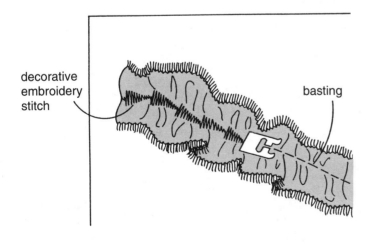

decorative embroidery stitch

basting

wf

Torn Strip Clusters

Stunning Fabric Strips

Margaret had fun with the torn-strip process as she embellished this green douppioni silk jacket. A complimentary color of green polyester, black and gold lacy nylon, and gold netting form the clustered compositions.

The green polyester is torn into strips and the edges were left unfinished. The nylon and netting are manually cut into strips. Each is stitched to the background fabric using the techniques in this chapter. The positioning of the strips is quite random. The finished result forms cluster groupings in various locations.

Clusters are completed with freehand stitching around their perimeter. Occasionally, bugle beads and sequins are sewn in place by hand.

To visually unify and join each cluster together, relief couching (Chapter 12) and a decorative machine stitch pattern are sewn to the background fabric.

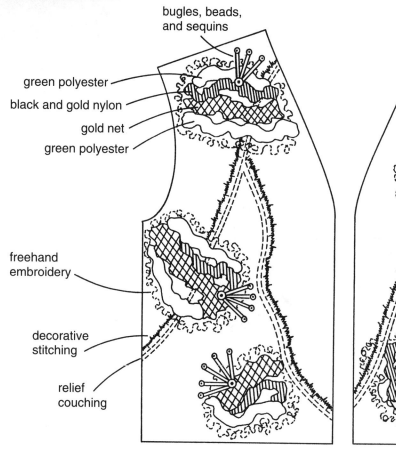
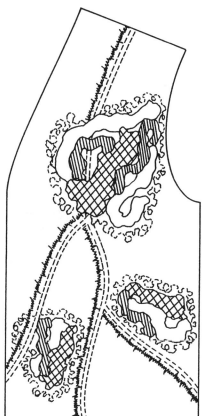

bugles, beads, and sequins

green polyester

black and gold nylon

gold net

green polyester

freehand embroidery

decorative stitching

relief couching

CHAPTER NINE

WOVEN MAGIC

WOVEN MAGIC is a special technique with double meaning. "Woven" suggests the predetermined interlocking of fabric strips in a variable woven pattern. "Magic" on the other hand means the random, free-flowing choice of colors and textures in the fabric strips that when woven together result in a striking work of unique beauty.

With this fabric manipulation technique, the torn strip–making process is simple and easy to do. However, the weaving and stitching process is more time consuming. Therefore, even though the result is incredibly beautiful and worth the effort, at first you may want to begin creating small amounts. This will help you learn the process and also will help you decide how much of it you want to create and where you'll use it in your garment.

I have used a Woven Magic fabric panel for the front of a vest. The vest back is constructed of plain satin. The entire vest is lined. The Project Page at the end of this chapter also offers a variation of woven magic used for yokes and cuffs. This finished weaving could also be made into any number of different accessories, like a handbag, or it could be a beautiful belt backed with stiff interfacing.

When doing the weaving, any number of different colors of fabric can be used; however, I recommend choosing a minimum of four different colors. In this vest, black, blue, green, and red were the primary colors chosen. These were a polyester, satin finished fabric. A multicolored organza which contained these primary colors, as well as yellow and orange, was also chosen. Gold lamé was also chosen to intersperse into the weaving. Your choices of colors will obviously change the outcome. A weaving of monochromatic colors will give a dramatically different outcome than shown here. Try pastels, try denims, try cottons — the choice is yours.

SPECIFIC
MATERIALS
AND SUPPLIES

- Fabric strips — compatible textures, different colors (a minimum of four, having similarities in thickness and weight)
- Organza fabric
- Thread
- Heavier decorative threads
- Metalfil or embroidery needle
- Rotary cutter and cutting mat
- Pin board, foam core board, or cardboard dressmaker's cutting board

METHOD

Preparing the Strips

1. When choosing fabrics to do your Woven Magic, select fabrics that tend to tear easily as most of our strips have torn edges. Also choose fabric colors that are compatible.

2. Tear the fabric into strips of varying widths from $1/2''$ (1.3 cm) to 1" (2.5 cm). You will be tearing from selvage to selvage — in other words, on the crosswise grain. How long your strips are and how many strips you have is completely optional. The longer they are and the more you have, the bigger your piece of Woven Magic will be. When tearing the strips, you'll often end up with long fibers that hang off the raw edge. Pull them away, keep the colors separate, store them in small plastic bags, and use them for a Mélange creation. See Chapter 11.

3. If the edges of the torn strips roll, press the strip flat. The edge is supposed to have a frayed effect.

4. If some of your fabrics do not tear well, cut the strips using the rotary cutter and mat.

5. If lamé fabric has been selected, note that it frays excessively when torn, it will therefore be prepared somewhat differently. Using the rotary cutter and cutting mat, cut strips of lamé approximately $1 1/2''$ (3.8 cm) wide. Fold right sides together the length of the strip. Stitch raw edge with $1/4''$ (.6 cm) seam to form a tube. Turn the tube right side out. Press the turned lamé strip with the seam in the middle of the underneath side.

6. You may want to shirr or ruche a few of the strips of fabric or lamé. Run a basting stitch down the center of the strip. Gently pull up on the gathering stitch to shirr or ruche the strip. This is only done to give a little additional texture, so keep the ruching to a minimum. You may want to lightly press each ruched strip before weaving it in.

7. Cut a piece of organza big enough to be the backing fabric. The size you cut the organza determines the approximate final size of the woven magic fabric panel that will be the end

PRO QUOTE

Making your own fabric with this woven magic process creates a fabric panel uniquely original to you.

result. Lay this on a pin board, large pressing table, or cardboard dressmaker's cutting board. Pin organza to the board around all four sides.

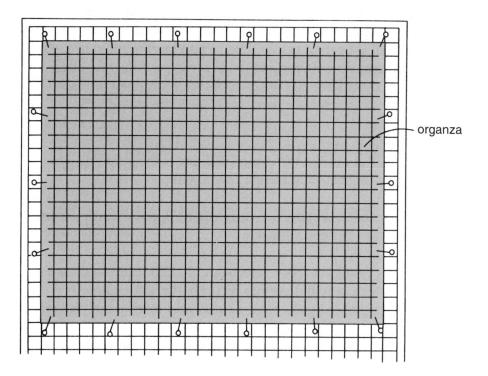

organza

PRO QUOTE

The weaving process is so simple to do. Vary the weaving pattern. Weave over one, under two. Weave over two, under two. Weave over three and under one. Whatever you do is perfectly all right.

Weaving the Strips

1. Take strip after strip of fabric and lay them down vertically over the organza-backing fabric on the pin board. Secure each strip side by side by pinning them into the organza-backing fabric. Your color placement can be as random as you wish.

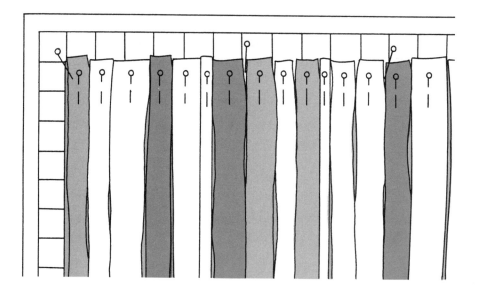

2. Remove the organza from the pin board. At the machine, sew a line of straight stitching across the top of all the torn strips to keep them in place on the organza.

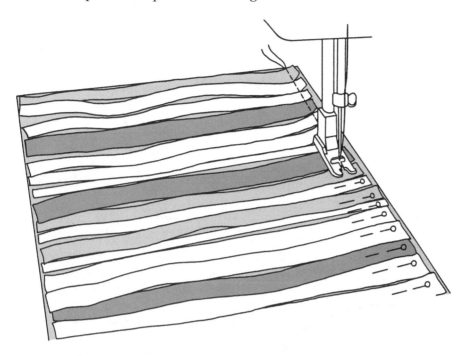

3. Lay organza, with strips attached, back onto the pin board. Pin organza into the board around all edges. To give stability to each strip before weaving, pin to board half way down each strip.

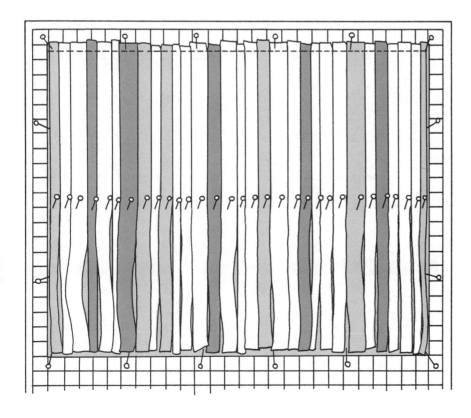

This woven magic fabric panel has become the bodice fronts of this stunning vest. The entire vest back, collar, and lining is sewn from complementary black satin. This is a unique wardrobe addition.

4. At the top, just below the stitching line, begin weaving in the horizontal strips of fabric. Once again, the colors that you use side by side are optional. The weaving process is also done randomly. You do not always have to go over one and under one strip. Vary the weaving. Sometimes go over two and under three vertical strips or over one and under two. To help in this horizontal weaving, attach a safety pin to the end of the strip.

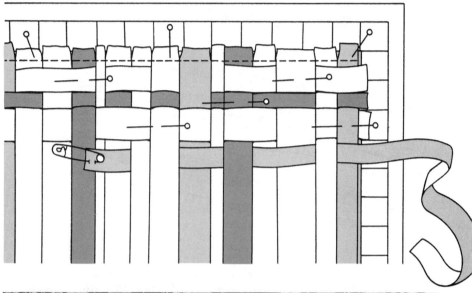

When creating your fabric panel from our woven magic process, remember that your weaving pattern can be completely random.

5. As you weave in each horizontal strip, secure it in place using many straight pins to temporarily attach it to the backing fabric.

6. Take the entire woven piece and backing fabric to the sewing machine and stitch around the three remaining outside edges using a straight stitch. You have now created the woven fabric panel.

stitch around outside edge

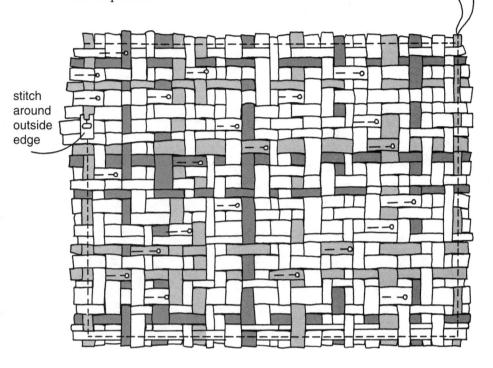

Stitching the Strips

The strips will now be stitched down to the backing fabric. Prepare your machine by inserting a metalfil or embroidery needle, loosen top tension, and use an embroidery foot. Use rayon or metallic threads on top. The bobbin thread color should match the backing fabric. Stitch the vertical strips first, then stitch the horizontal strips. Choose a straight stitch, a triple straight stitch, or a simple pattern incorporating a straight stitch.

1. Using rayon or metallic threads, begin stitching the vertical strips on the right-hand side of the fabric panel. Stitch from top to bottom down the middle of the strip using varying stitch patterns of your choice. Any straight stitch, light open patterns, or a few heavier satin stitch patterns are appropriate. Stitch from strip to strip, occasionally leaving

some strips unstitched so that you can come back later and cable stitch them. See Chapter 12 for cable stitching technique. End on the left-hand side of the fabric panel.

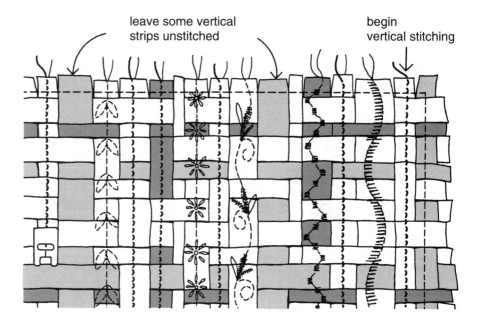

Note: Make sure you always stitch in the same direction, that is from top to bottom. This way, if there is any puckering or movement of the strips, it will always move in the same direction. Put your hands flat on the woven piece and use your fingers to help guide the sewing of each strip.

2. Use a variety of straight stitch patterns and thread colors and stitch down the middle of the horizontal strips securing them to the backing fabric. Again, turn the weaving so that you work from the right side and stitch toward the left side. Make sure as you stitch across the vertical strips that the

edges do not get pushed under the presser foot and get rolled over and stitched on themselves. Keep the vertical strips as flat as possible. Again, you will want to leave some of the horizontal strips unstitched and ready for cable stitching.

leave some horizontal
strips unstitched

turn and begin
horizontal stitching

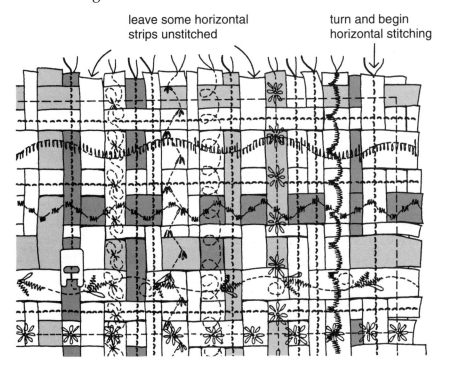

Decorating the Strips with Cable Stitching

It is now time to apply the heavier decorative threads using cable stitching. Since they will be too heavy to go through the eye of the needle, they must be wound on the bobbin. The thread used on the top of the machine must be the same color (or close to the color) as the heavy thread on the bobbin. Since this is cable stitching, the woven piece is turned over so that the right side is face down. However, because the organza is see–through, you'll be able to see the strips that you'll stitch on. See Chapter 12 for more details on cable stitching.

Jenny has created a woven magic fabric panel and used it to cut the yokes and cuffs for her black microfiber blouse.

3. Now go back to the vertical and horizontal strips that you left unstitched and begin attaching them with cable stitching. To prevent the machine from jamming, choose stitch patterns that are relatively open and constructed of straight stitches.

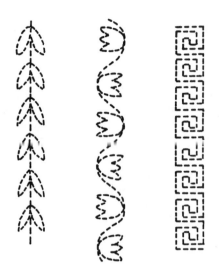

Some open stitch patterns
suitable for cable stitching.

4. Stitch your chosen vertical strips first, working from right to left.

5. Stitch your chosen horizontal strips next. Stitch these working from right to left.

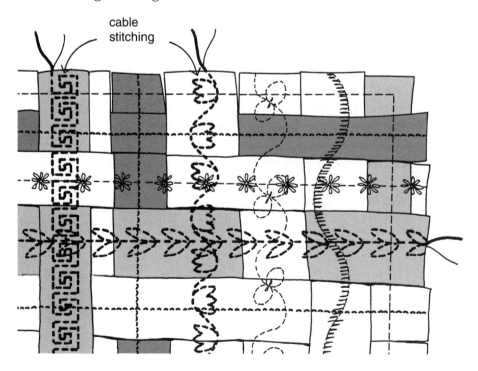

cable
stitching

Here are two excellent ways to use your woven magic fabric panel — as a special effect for yokes and cuffs, and for the fronts of a vest.

Since this created fabric panel was not stabilized or stitched in the hoop, the panel will *shrink* somewhat. It may develop a slight amount of puckering; however, this should disappear when pressed. Remember, when pressing, to protect the strips by use of a press cloth.

Woven Magic

If the process of Woven Magic intrigues you, a possible application of the woven fabric panel is to use it as front and back yoke and cuffs for a blouse. Jenny Anastas did just that.

Additionally, you might want to sew an accompanying handbag. Any size of bag can be sewn. Simply change the dimensions to suit your needs. This bag finishes 12″ (30.5 cm) wide by 7″ (18 cm) deep.

1. For the outside of the bag, begin with a rectangle of 13 $\frac{1}{4}$″ (34 cm) wide by 20 $\frac{1}{4}$″ (52 cm) long. Round one end of the rectangle that will become the flap. For the lining, cut one piece of lining fabric the same dimensions as the outside. To stiffen the bag, apply one or two layers of *very* stiff iron–on interfacing to the wrong side of the outside of the bag. Alternatively, cut a piece of buckram the shape of the bag. Sew it to the wrong side of the woven magic.

2. With right sides together, fold outside of bag up 7 $\frac{5}{8}$″ (19.3 cm). Stitch each side with $\frac{5}{8}$″ (1.6 cm) seam. Fold up and stitch sides of lining in the same manner. Turn bag right side out.

3. With right sides together, put bag inside lining making sure to line up side seams. Stitch curved flap of lining and bag together starting where you ended the side seam stitching and ending when you reach the other side seam.

4. Turn lining to inside of bag. On remaining open edge, fold in $\frac{5}{8}$″ (1.6 cm) seam allowances of both bag and lining. Top stitch to close seam. Determine placement for the Velcro™ closure. Velcro can be stitched by machine to the inside edge of the bag. For the flap, use a fabric/ Velcro glue to secure the Velcro to the flap.

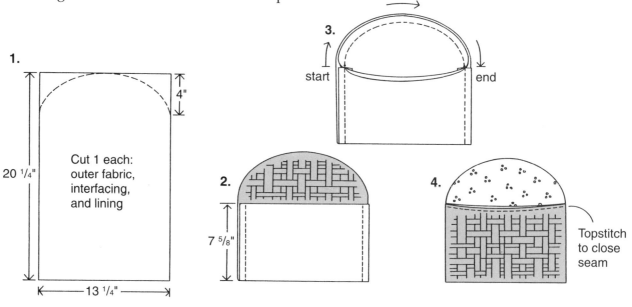

1.

4″

20 $\frac{1}{4}$″

Cut 1 each:
outer fabric,
interfacing,
and lining

13 $\frac{1}{4}$″

2.

7 $\frac{5}{8}$″

3.

start   end

4.

Topstitch
to close
seam

CHAPTER TEN

PIN TUCKING AND CONCERTINA TUCKING

PIN TUCKING AND CONCERTINA TUCKING are easy and simple methods used to manipulate the surface of the fabric. Concertina tucking is a simple variation on regular pin tucking. They both use twin needle stitching (where the two needle threads are pulled gently together with the single bobbin thread). A raised ridge of fabric is created when the bobbin thread draws the two top threads together thereby forming the pin tuck. Very little fabric is pulled into this pin tuck; however, when stitching multiple tucks, some fabric "shrinkage" will occur. Be mindful of this when choosing the area or detail to be embellished with pin tucks or concertina tucks.

SUGGESTED
APPLICATION
AND USAGE

Pin tucking is created when a fold of fabric is stitched close to the fold. Multiple pin tucks simply mean many folds are stitched, often in parallel rows. With regular pin tucking, all folds occur on the top or right side of the fabric.

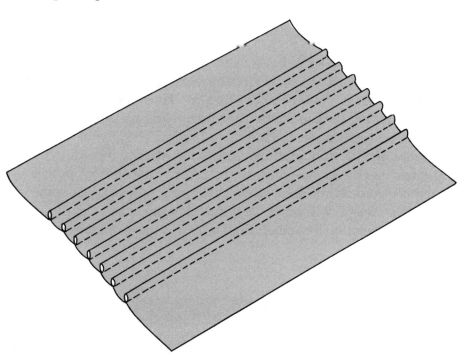

Concertina tucking is when the first fold and stitching occurs on the right side and the second fold and stitching will be done on the *wrong* side of the fabric. In other words, the fabric is turned over to the wrong side and then the pin tuck is stitched there.

PRO QUOTE

Twin needles are available in varying widths. The narrower the space between the needles, the tighter and smaller the finished tuck will be.

Therefore, you first pin tuck the right side, then turn the fabric over and tuck wrong side. This right side–wrong side pattern is repeated to form the manipulated fabric.

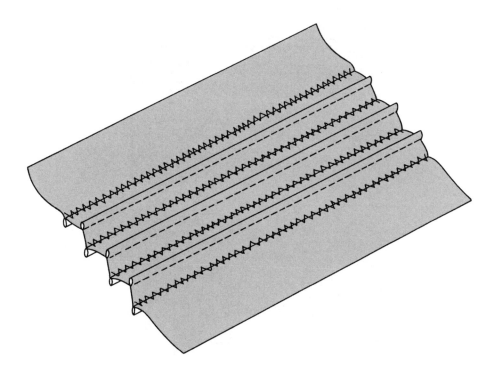

Pin tucking could be done with hand stitches; however few seamstresses will spend the time to do that when we have the availability of twin needles and pin tucking, or cording feet for our sewing machines.

Once the regular pin tucks or concertina tucks are completed, the fabric can be used as is to be cut as an entire pattern piece such as a yoke, cuff, collar, or pocket — or perhaps the bodice of an evening gown.

The tucked piece could also be cut in odd shapes and used to embellish a jacket, vest, or blouse. See the fuchsia–black–gold vest in Chapter 15 where concertina tucks are featured in one section.

Pro Quote

If a bobbin seems snug and the thread is not flowing freely through the tension gauge, check for fuzz jammed between the bobbin and case or for very small thread bits wedged between the bobbin and the case.

Also, depending on what project you want to sew, vertical tucks can be crossed with stitched horizontal tucks to create designs well suited for corners of placements, napkins, or pot holders.

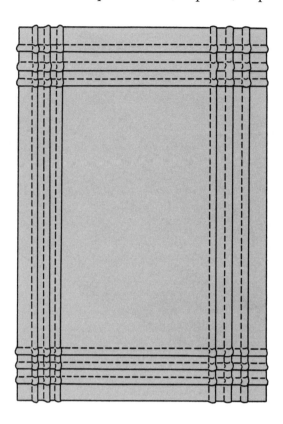

SPECIFIC
MATERIALS
AND SUPPLIES

PRO QUOTE

It's handier to have duplicate specialty needles, so if there's a problem with one you don't have to interupt your work to run to the store for another one.

• Twin (double) needle — a needle where two needles hang down from a single shank. These needles come in a variety of widths and spaces between the needles. This space is measured in millimeters. Most machines that have a zigzag stitch have a wide needle opening in the throat plate that will accommodate a twin needle.

• Pin-tucking or cording foot — your machine will most likely
have a pin-tucking or cording foot available for your model. A
cording foot generally has only one groove on the underside.
Pin-tucking feet come with a variety of grooves on the
underside. With less grooves, the tucked space is wider; with
more grooves, the tucked space is narrower. If you have choices,
experiment with both because they each provide different final
effects.

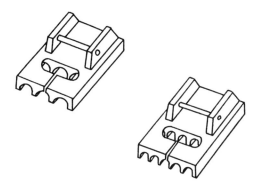

• Thread — choose threads that are compatible with the desired
finished look. Metallic, rayon, embroidery, or good-quality
sewing threads can be used. Threads contrasting in color with
the base fabric will produce a different effect than using threads
of a blending or similar color. The choice is yours.

Threading the Machine

If you want two spools of the same color thread on the top of the
machine, and you only have one spool of that thread color, simply
fill a bobbin with the same thread and use it as the second spool.
To prevent tangling, threads *must* be separated as they come off
the spools so that they have an individual path down to the
needles.

Machines with Upright Spool Holders

1. Thread on the left spool holder will unwind from the left
    side.

2. Thread it through the lower side of the tension gauge, then
    through the thread take–up lever.

MACHINE SET–UP

PRO QUOTE

*When threading the
machine for twin
needle stitching, the
threads must unwind
in opposite directions
so that they are
separated and will
have an individual
path down
to the needles.*

3. Left-side thread is threaded through the left needle.

4. The spool on the right must unwind from the right side.

5. Thread it through the upper side of the tension gauge, then through the thread take–up lever.

6. Right-side thread is then threaded through the right-side needle.

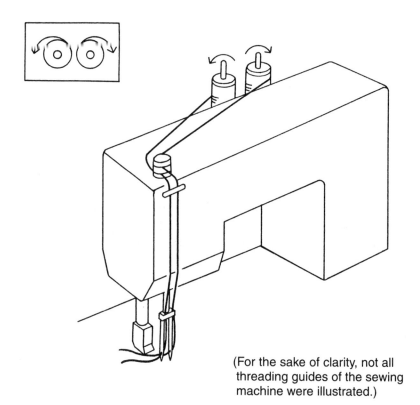

(For the sake of clarity, not all threading guides of the sewing machine were illustrated.)

PRO QUOTE

When stitching with a twin needle, the sewing machine throat plate must have a needle hole wide enough for both needles to pass through at one time.

Machines with Horizontal Spool Holders

1. The spool of thread on the bottom level will unwind from the back side up.

2. Thread it through the left side of the thread tension gauge, and then through the thread take–up lever.

3. Thread the bottom-level thread through the left-side needle.

4. The spool of thread on the upper level will unwind from the front side up.

5. Thread it through the right side of the tension gauge and then through the thread take–up lever.

6. Thread the upper-level thread through the right-side needle.

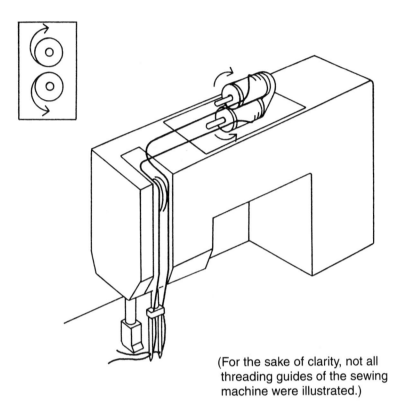

(For the sake of clarity, not all threading guides of the sewing machine were illustrated.)

PRO QUOTE

When using a twin needle, if the thread is always breaking on one side only, discard the needle and get a new one.

METHOD

Pin Tucking

1. After threading the machine and twin needles, and making certain that the pin tucking foot is in place, do a test sample. The tension on the needle threads may need to be tightened slightly so that the underside or bobbin side of the fabric looks like an even hand stem stitch. Experiment with the effect and look you like.

2. To ensure that tucks are evenly spaced on the fabric, always fold the fabric in half and press a crease down the center.

3. Begin the first row of pin tuck stitching on the crease line. The left-side needle will stitch on the left side of the crease. The right-side needle will stitch on the right side of the crease.

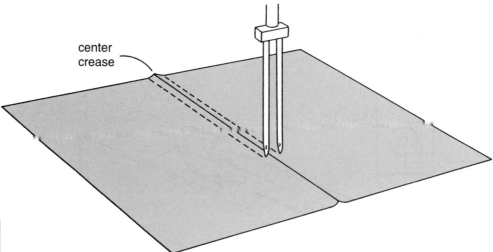

center crease

4. For the second row, stitch on the right side of the first row of tucking. For the third row, stitch on the left side of the first or center row of tucking. Always stitch from top to bottom (in the same direction which eliminates fabric pulling and puckering between the pin tucks, that is).

5. Always alternate from right to left side of the first center row of stitching. This ensures uniformity and symmetry on the final product.

Regular pin tucks are stitched ¼" apart on the yoke of this blouse. Decorative machine stitched tucks were sewn on the chambray and then the triangular shapes were cut and appliquéd onto the yoke.

Concertina Tucking

1. Follow all the above-mentioned procedures for preparing and sewing pin tucks. However, after the first or center tucked row is stitched, turn the fabric over to the wrong side. The next rows of stitching on the right and left of the center row will be sewn on the wrong side.

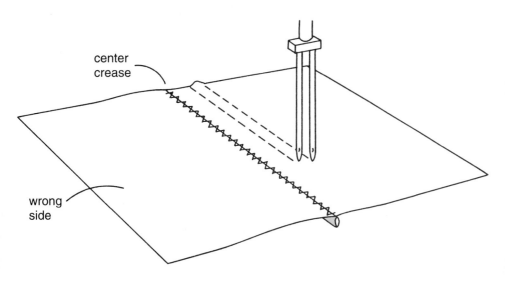

2. The fourth and fifth rows of stitching will be done on the *right* side of the fabric.

3. The sixth and seventh rows of stitching will be done on the *wrong* side of the fabric.

4. By stitching alternately from the right side to the wrong side of the fabric, the resulting effect will be much like accordion bellows that go in and out — hence the name, "Concertina tucking."

5. Once again, experiment with right and wrong side pin tucking. You may prefer two tucks stitched on the right side and only one tuck on the wrong side. In other words, create you own pattern.

6. Depending on the fabric's gloss or sheen, this stitching can create a very dramatic effect.

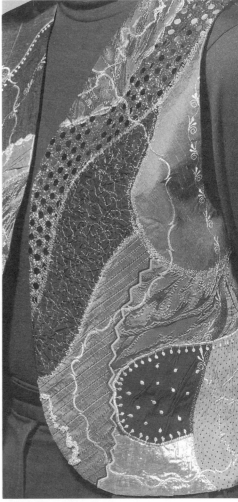

Glenda's fuchsia–gold–black vest, featured in the color plates, has incorporated many different Fabriqué™ techniques. The area of interest in this photo is the appliqué shape that was texturized with concertina tucking.

Further Fabric Manipulation

- The tucked fabric could also be further manipulated by any of the scrunching techniques. See Chapter 7 on Scrunching. It could then be cut to the desired shape and appliquéd to the garment as an embellishment.

- Try pin tucking over the pin-tucked fabric by stitching at right angles or diagonally across existing rows of tucks.

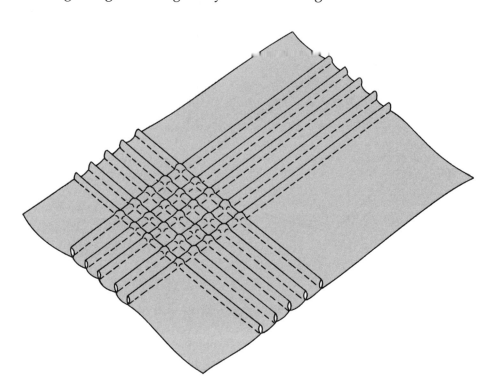

- To form decoratively patterned pin tucks, try pin tucking with open straight stitch-type patterns from your sewing machine. Be careful if the stitch patterns are quite wide as the opening in the pin tuck foot may not be wide enough for the total width of the stitch pattern. Some machines have a button that, when engaged, will ensure that the decorative stitch pattern will not stitch too wide, which would prevent the needle from swinging too wide and breaking.

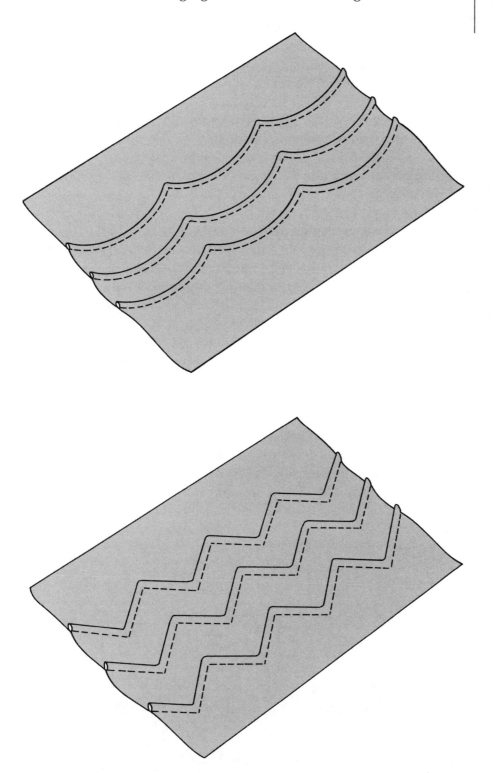

Pin-Tucked Blouse

Pin Tucking and Concertina Tucking

I had fun preparing and sewing this chambray, pin-tucked, embellished blouse. Choose any simple shirt pattern with a yoke. Cut the yoke pattern at least 1" (2.5 cm) larger around all edges. This allows for any fabric *shrinkage* that may occur while pin tucking. Using this enlarged pattern as a guide, cut a rectangle of fabric the width and length of the pattern piece.

Next begin pin-tucking the background yoke fabric. Use thread color that matches the fabric. Stitch 22 rows of pin tucks each 1/4" (.6 cm) apart from side to side across the yoke area. You can pin tuck as many rows as you wish depending on the depth of your yoke.

To form the triangle appliqué shapes, cut a piece of background fabric 12" (31 cm) x 8" (21 cm). Straight-stitched tucks should be alternated with decorative stitch pattern tucks until the entire rectangle is tucked. I call this the "wallpaper" piece.

Draw three large and three small triangles. Cut the triangle shapes out of the pin-tucked wall paper. Cut triangular holes out of the large triangles. Decide where you want the large and small triangles to be placed. Appliqué these shapes onto the background fabric. Satin stitch around the appliqué shapes.

Further embellishment can then be added. I couched on a double thickness of metallic yarn. See Chapter 12 on Couching. The couching pattern is random and yet it repeats the angles and points formed by the triangles. Sequins and bugle beads further enhance this project. Once all embellishment is completed, cut yoke to original pattern size and shape.

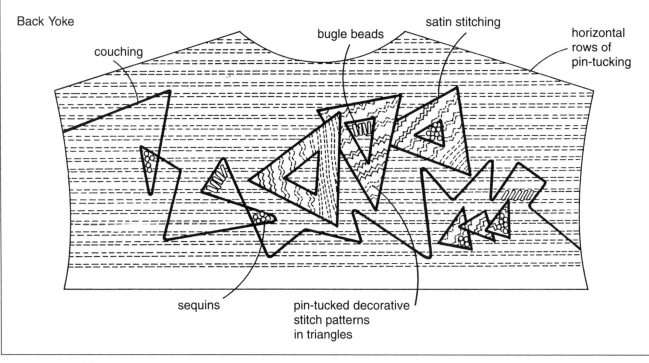

Back Yoke

couching

bugle beads

satin stitching

horizontal rows of pin-tucking

sequins

pin-tucked decorative stitch patterns in triangles

FABRIQUÉ™ MÉLANGE

MÉLANGE...what a delightful word! Mélange means to create, mix, blend, and develop your own fabric. We describe three different techniques to develop your fabric mélange. For all three methods, bits of threads and fibers; tiny pieces of ribbon, cord, or other trim; or shreds of fabric are "sandwiched" between stabilizing material, freehand stitched together and used as a *piece of fabric* for embellishment. None of these fabric mélange methods take long to do; therefore I recommend trying a sample of each. You'll not only realize how easy this process is, but you will also discover the different weights of mélange that you can create.

**SUGGESTED
APPLICATION
AND USAGE**

In doing your different test samples, let your imagination wander. I know you'll come up with wonderful creations and ideas for a variety of ways to use your final mélange creation. If you haven't started already, remember to save all your thread and fabric scraps for a creative project such as Fabriqué™ Mélange. When thread becomes jammed up, tangled, and totally unusable, don't throw it out — keep it for working a mélange.

**SUGGESTED
APPLICATION
AND USAGE**

Fabriqué™ Mélange can be created into differing weights. The more thread, fibers, and trims that are used, the thicker the fabric will become. Method 2 creates a more stable and somewhat rigid mélange because fusible webbing is pressed onto the backing surface. Therefore, it is best used in something like a wall hanging, soft furnishings, or in a purse or eyeglasses case that could be covered with stitch–through plastic.

Since Methods 1 and 2 do not require fusible webbing, the resulting mélange is more pliable and looks wonderful in a yoke or as a cuff, or further manipulated by gathering an edge and using it as a raised relief element on a finished garment.

**SPECIFIC
MATERIALS
AND SUPPLIES**

• Organza fabric
• Decorative thread
• Ribbon, cord, or trims
• Fabric bits
• Metallic thread
• Water–soluble fabric stabilizer
• Paper–backed fusible webbing
• Embroidery hoop
• Darning foot
• Appliqué mat

METHODS

Method 1

1. On a piece of see-through, lightweight fabric, such as organza (this becomes the backing fabric), drop cut up pieces of threads (rayon and metallic threads are wonderful), tiny pieces of ribbon, or other flat cording or trim. You could also

drop yarns or fibers from your favorite knitting supply. All bits and pieces are dropped randomly on top of the base fabric.

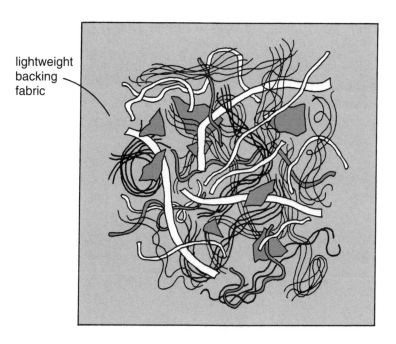

lightweight backing fabric

The more bits and pieces that are dropped on the base fabric, the more dense the finished fabric will be. Try to develop an even distribution of these bits and pieces over the surface of the organza.

2. Cut a piece of water–soluble fabric stabilizer large enough to cover the organza and thread bits.

3. Place the layers securely in an embroidery hoop.

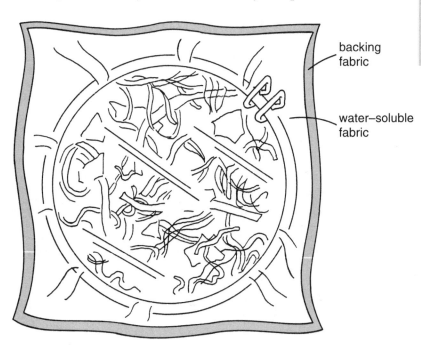

backing fabric

water–soluble fabric

PRO QUOTE

No need to throw out anything any more! Save all your leftover bits of thread, fabric scraps, trims and yarns. All will come in handy when creating Fabriqué™ Mélange.

4. Set the machine for freehand embroidery. See Chapter 5 on Freehand Embroidery. Have the darning foot placed on the machine.

5. With complimentary embroidery thread on the machine, top and bobbin, begin random freehand stitching within the hoop. I like to call this "scribble stitching." There must be enough stitches throughout so that when the water–soluble fabric is dissolved, all bits and pieces will remain in place and not fall apart once the water–soluble stabilizer is washed away.

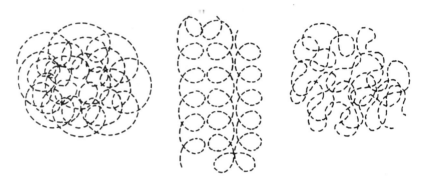

freehand stitch patterns — "scribble stitching"

Threads used for this freehand embroidery can be changed to different compatible color combinations. Couching of various metallic or other complimentary yarns or ribbons could further be sewn on top to embellish the surface. If the thread is too heavy to go on the top of the machine, wind the thread on the bobbin and continue stitching from the underside of the fabric. This is often referred to as cable stitching. See Chapter 12 on Couching, Cable Stitching, and Dribbling.

6. When enough free stitching has been done to secure all sandwiched "bits," dip the mélange in water (follow manufacturer's directions) to dissolve the water–soluble fabric layer. Before dipping in water, cut away any excess soluble fabric and save for future use.

7. Air dry the mélange.

8. You have now created a beautiful piece of Fabriqué™ Mélange. When completely dry, it can be used for yokes, cuffs, or pockets. See The Project Page at the end of this chapter for details on creating the organza blouse. Or, you can use it as a piece of fabric incorporated into a final media mix of manipulated fabric comprising a total garment.

Method 2

1. On a piece of very lightweight backing fabric, like organza, iron on paper-backed fusible webbing. Place the fusible side down on right side of fabric.

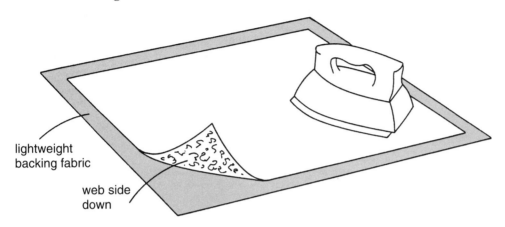

lightweight
backing fabric

web side
down

2. Fuse in place with steam iron.

3. Remove paper backing from fusible webbing.

4. Drop bits and pieces of complimentary threads, yarns, ribbons, trims, and fabric onto fusible web.

5. Using an appliqué mat, place it on top of all the threads and bits and pieces. Press to fuse the threads and other yarns and bits to the backing fabric.

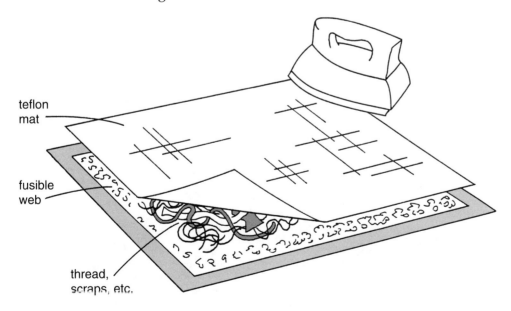

teflon
mat

fusible
web

thread,
scraps, etc.

6. Top this layer with a piece of water–soluble fabric.

7. Place all these layers securely in an embroidery hoop.

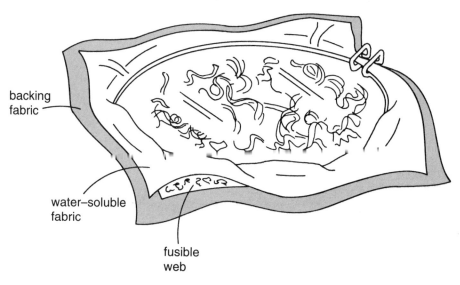

backing fabric

water–soluble fabric

fusible web

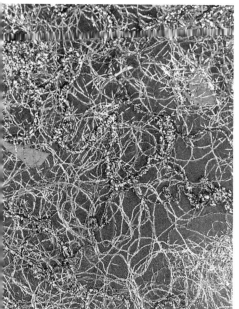

This close-up provides a look at some of the detail on our Fabriqué™ Mélange. Delicate "dribbling" (see Chapter 12) is stitched onto the surface of the finished creation.

8. Set machine for freehand embroidery, making sure that the darning foot is attached and the feed dog is lowered or covered. See Chapter 5 on Freehand Embroidery.

9. Freehand in a random stitch pattern (scribble stitch) with compatible threads to secure all threads and other pieces.

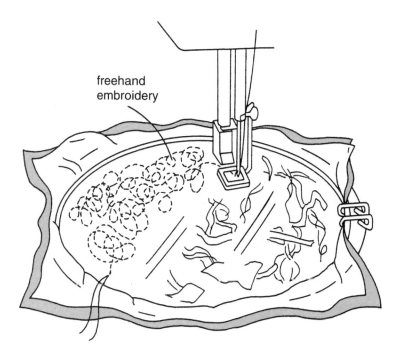

freehand embroidery

10. Add other embellishments such as couched cords, yarns or trims. Try experimenting by appliquéing on additional fabric shapes like leaves, flowers, etc. There must be enough total stitching to secure all fiber contents originally "sandwiched" between the two layers.

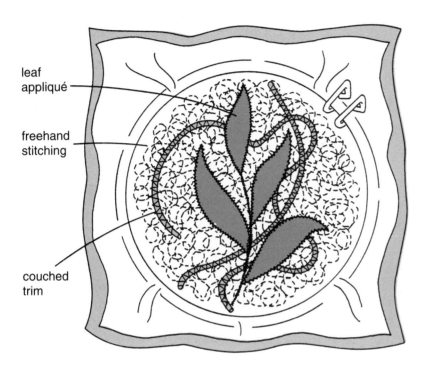

leaf
appliqué

freehand
stitching

couched
trim

11. Trim away excess water–soluble fabric from the perimeter of the stitching. Dissolve water–soluble fabric away in water.

12. Because this method results in stiffer fabric, it would be appropriate to use for cuffs and yokes as well as in wall hangings and other home deco projects.

Method 3

1. Use water–soluble fabric as the backing material. Organza is not used in this method.

2. Drop cut up pieces of thread and other bits of ribbon and yarns onto the water–soluble fabric. This "thread" layer can be fairly dense or as sparse as you like, as long as it covers the backing fabric evenly.

3. Top this thread layer with another piece of water–soluble fabric.

4. Secure all layers in the embroidery hoop.

two layers of water–soluble fabric

5. Set machine for freehand embroidery stitching. Make sure the darning foot is on the machine, and the feed dog is lowered or covered. See Chapter 5 on Freehand Embroidery.

6. Random freehand straight stitch (scribble stitch) through all layers. Make sure all stitching lines overlap and cross each other. Again, use compatible threads. Different colors of threads can be used as desired. Enough freehand embroidery stitching must be done in order to secure the "thread" layer. If not enough stitching is done, it will fall apart when dissolved; therefore, make sure that the stitching often doubles back and crosses over itself.

7. Add any other embellishing of couched cords or yarns.

8. Trim away any excess water–soluble fabric from the edges, then dissolve the water–soluble fabric in water.

9. Air dry completely.

PRO QUOTE

Trim away excess water–soluble fabric from the work before dissolving in water. Otherwise it creates a rather sticky, gelatinous mess in the sink.

10. You are now left with a magnificent new piece of fabric mélange that is made solely of threads, fabric bits, fibers, and yarns with no backing fabric. It can now be incorporated into your finished garment. You can cut your designs in random shapes, bond with paper backed fusible webbing, peel off the paper, and then bond to the background fabric. It would generally be further stitched in place either with four or five rows of freehand serpentine stitch or if your machine has an open cornelly stitch, that would be suitable to use on the cut edge.

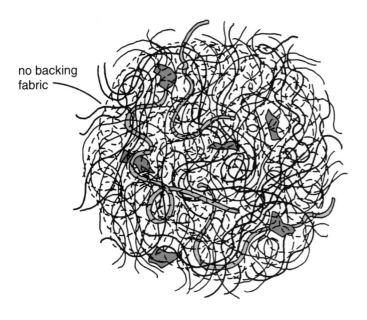

no backing fabric

Water–Soluble Fabric — Information and Characteristics

• Man-made spun alginate solution
• Fabric is stretchy and fragile
• Tears easily
• May need to use a double layer of it for stability
• Using a ball–point needle helps to prevent fabric tearing
• Thread tension should be even on both top and bottom
• Before dissolving away, cut off excess fabric around the design

PRO QUOTE

Water–soluble fabric stabilizer is a man–made spun alginate solution which is stretchy and fragile. After stitching is completed, excess dissolves away in water.

Mélange Blouse

Fabriqué™ Mélange

Jenny Anastas created this beautiful piece of Fabriqué™ Mélange using Method 1 as described in this chapter. This mélange is beautifully enhanced with dribbling stitched with a lightweight, gold yarn as described in Chapter 12. To design the blouse pattern, I used the Sure–Fit Designs™ Shirt Kit which does not have a bust fitting dart. The fabric chosen is elegant organza, which is the backing fabric for the mélange and also the main body of the blouse.

Since this piece of mélange is so elegant and stunning, I chose to cut the yokes and cuffs from it, thereby keeping the pattern design simple to show off the beauty of the work.

Since I wanted to have a minimum of seams, I drew the front and back yokes joined together without any shoulder seams. The front and back yoke pattern is cut from the mélange. Again, to avoid unsightly seams in the organza, I cut a full bodice front and back and simply laid the mélange yoke over top of the shoulder area. Straight stitching secured the yoke to the blouse at center front, neck edge, and armhole seams. The raw edge of the mélange yoke is stitched to the bodice using a simple satin stitch done with gold thread.

I was fortunate to find small, gold ball buttons that had a surface texture that looked like the dribbling that was done on the mélange. They are an excellent complement to complete this stunning blouse.

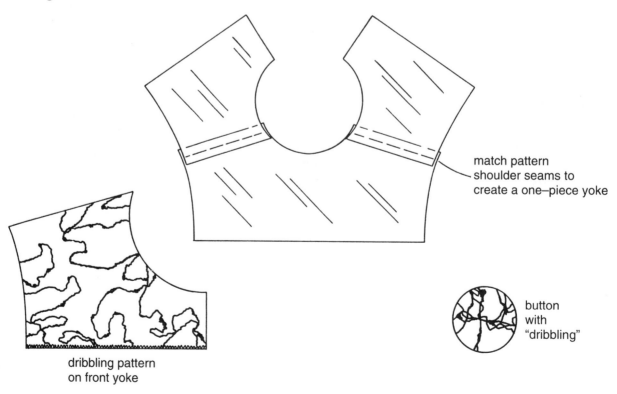

match pattern
shoulder seams to
create a one–piece yoke

dribbling pattern
on front yoke

button
with
"dribbling"

COUCHING, CABLE STITCHING, AND DRIBBLING

COUCHING, CABLE STITCHING, AND DRIBBLING are forms of embellishment that attach a cord, yarn, thread, or group of threads onto the surface of the fabric with stitches or stitch groupings. Stitching can be done by hand or by machine. Here the focus will be on stitching by machine.

SUGGESTED APPLICATION AND USAGE

Whichever method you choose for applying a heavier thread, yarn, cord, or braid, all can add considerable depth and impact to the finished project. Many specific areas of a garment, like the bodice, shoulder, yoke, cuffs, or collars, could be decorated with these embellishment techniques. Fashion accessories such as handbags, belts, and eyeglasses cases could also be couched, cable stitched, or dribbled. Any specific pattern shape like flowers, leaves, or butterflies, can be transferred to the fabric. From specific shapes, let your creativity move into geometric patterns and shapes, and from there to totally abstract placement of the embellishment.

SPECIFIC MATERIALS AND SUPPLIES

• Fabric
• Decorative thread, cord, embroidery floss, braid, or yarn
• Heavyweight machine yarns and threads
• Twin (double) needle
• Metalfil needle
• Fabric stabilizer
• Cording foot
• Darning foot
• Embroidery hoop

METHOD

Couching

Any kind of cord, embroidery floss, braid, or yarns can be attached to the fabric. When they are laid on the right side of the fabric and stitched over the top with a zigzag stitch, that is referred to as surface couching.

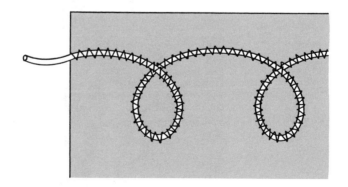

PRO QUOTE

To ensure that the trim will be evenly stitched and if you don't have a cording foot, hold the yarn or trim up at a 45° angle in front of the needle while stitching over it.

You may want to attach a cording foot onto your machine. This foot generally has a hole or a slot in the front where the trim is fed through. Otherwise, hold the trim up at a 45° angle in front of the needle when stitching over it. This ensures that the trim will be stitched evenly.

If the design to be couched is a specific shape or pattern, transfer the pattern lines onto the background fabric by using dressmaker's chalk or a water–soluble or disappearing marking pencil. Any marked area that does not get covered by the trim and stitching will then be much easier to remove.

If your design has tight corners or lots of curves, make sure to use a narrow, flexible trim. Wider trim is much more easily applied onto straight lines or gently flowing curves.

Stitch a sample of the trim to the background fabric. If any puckering occurs, you will need to stabilize the fabric before couching on the trim. Use any tear–away stabilizer or secure the background fabric in an embroidery hoop.

To finish the end of a couched trim, enclose it in a seam if you can. Using a large–eyed needle, feed the trim to the wrong side. Or clip the trim close to the stitching and apply a dot of liquid seam sealant.

A couching sampler. When yarns, threads, or cords are too heavy to go through the eye of the needle or be wound on the bobbin, they are laid on the fabric's surface and stitched over the top to hold them in place.

Swing Couching

Swing couching is a variation on regular surface couching. You will be swinging and wiggling the trim back and forth as you stitch over it. Therefore, you must use a very soft, flexible, and pliable braid, trim, or cord. Because you will be swinging the trim back and forth, use a fairly wide zigzag stitch, or try sewing over the top with various open and decorative machine stitch patterns to create your desired effect.

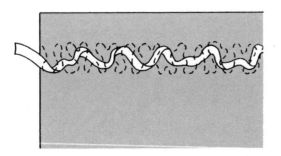

Margaret applied the techniques of couching and cable stitching on her red matador jacket. For a detailed outline of the stitches and pattern turn to the Project Page at the end of this chapter.

PRO QUOTE

With cable stitching, heavy threads, cords and yarns are wound on the bobbin and the work is sewn with the right side of the fabric facing down.

Relief Couching

Yarn or cord is placed under the fabric and is stitched to the fabric. A twin (double) needle is used in the machine. When sewing, the needles straddle either side of the cord and will produce a raised effect on the right side of the fabric. Make sure the twin (double) needles are spaced far enough apart to straddle the diameter of the cord.

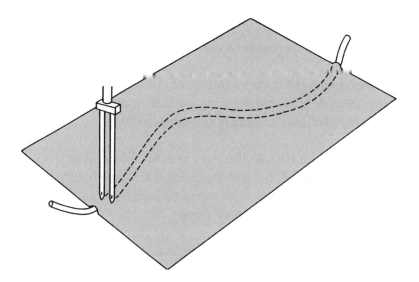

Use a knit edge or cording foot on the machine and lower the top thread tension.

With any kind of couching, the threads you choose for the upper and bobbin threads will affect the final result. If you want the thread to be an integral part of the final effect, use a thread color that matches the fabric or a clear monofilament thread. If you want to add contrast, choose a contrasting color or a metallic thread.

Cable Stitching

If you want the yarn or cord to be a part of the sewing machine stitch and the cord, yarn or thread is too thick to go through the eye of the needle, wind it on the bobbin and stitch from the underside of the fabric. This is generally referred to as "cable stitching."

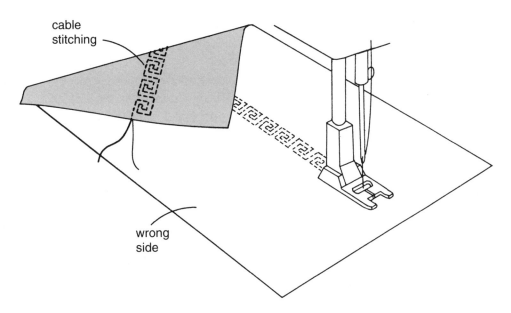

cable
stitching

wrong
side

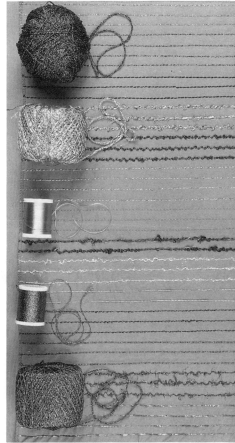

A cable stitching sampler. When threads or fine yarns are too heavy to go through the eye of the needle, wind them on the bobbin, then stitch them directly onto the fabric's surface.

Because the yarn, cord, or heavy thread is on the bobbin, it can either pass through the bobbin tension gauge or it can bypass the bobbin tension altogether. If the cord goes through the bobbin, you will likely need to decrease the bobbin tension. Most bobbin cases have some type of tension screw. When you turn it to the left, you loosen the tension; when you turn it to the right, you tighten. If you are concerned about doing this and then resetting the tension for normal stitching, a safe way to overcome this problem is to buy a second bobbin case and mark it with bright nail polish. Then you can play around and adjust the bobbin tension all you want and not worry about returning it to the proper straight–stitching tension. If you do any amount of this type of stitching, the minor financial investment is worth it.

Once again, I highly recommend doing sample work before you embellish your finished garment or fabric art piece. Try stitching the heavy yarn by using a loosened bobbin tension. Then do a sample and bypass the bobbin tension altogether. Try straight stitching, zigzagging, and decorative machine embroidery stitches. Do not satin stitch, as it often produces too much bulk and will cause thread build up and jamming. These will all be done with a stabilizer (such as placing the work in an embroidery

PRO QUOTE

Dribbling, a form of cable stitching, is done where the bobbin thread by–passes the bobbin tension completely. The result — wonderful, three dimensional, textured stitching is formed on the right side.

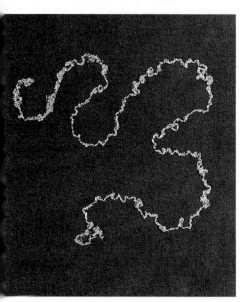

Dribbling can take on many final forms and shapes. Here is a close-up of dribbling randomly wandering over the fabric.

hoop), with the feed dog in regular raised or stitching position and the embroidery or regular sewing foot in place on the machine. Now you're ready to go on to dribbling, which is cable stitching done with freehand embroidery.

Dribbling

Dribbling is a form of cable stitching. Heavier and decorative threads or yarns that are too thick to pass through the eye of the needle are wound on the bobbin; however, with dribbling, the thread or yarn is placed in the bobbin case and the tension gauge is *bypassed* completely. The bobbin thread or yarn is then pulled up through the throat plate. The fabric is stitched with the wrong side up and the bobbin "thread" creates the raised, lumpy textured stitching on the right side of the fabric. What you are doing is laying the bobbin thread on the surface of the right side of the fabric thereby creating wonderful three-dimensional textural patterns and designs.

I just love the effect of dribbling on embellished garments. It's free–form. It's erratic. It can be glitzy and eye–catching depending on the colors of threads and yarns used on the final fabric. My favorite "yarn" to use can be found in a knitting and wool shop and is sometimes referred to as *gold fingering* (not a brand name). It is a fine yet somewhat nubby textured yarn that comes in gold and silver as well as in many metallic colors like green, blue, or red. In machine and fabric stores look for thread called "candlelight." Experiment with different weights and colors of yarns and threads available to you and see the variety of effects you can create.

1.   Wind the machine bobbin with heavy threads (embroidery) or fine yet strong yarns (gold or silver yarns, for example). You can wind the bobbin by machine or you can *hand* wind the bobbin. When winding by machine, do not run the machine too fast or the yarn could jump out of the bobbin and wind around the bobbin shaft. Watch that you don't overfill the bobbin or it will not fit in the case. Be aware that this form of stitching uses up the bobbin fill very rapidly. Be prepared to keep refilling the bobbin as needed.

2.   Place the bobbin in the bobbin case.

3. Bypass the bobbin thread tension guide completely. You may need to check your machine's owner's manual to find out the proper procedure.

4. Bring the bobbin thread or yarn up through throat plate.

5. The upper thread on the machine must be in a similar or matching color, (gold thread for gold yarn, for example). You may want to use a large–eyed needle like a size 14/90 or 12/80; however, if you have metallic thread on the top side, use a metalfil needle.

6. Because you are going to stitch with freehand embroidery, lower or cover the feed dog.

7. Set the machine for regular straight stitching.

8. Upper thread tension may need to be increased; however, I strongly recommend that you do a sample of this stitching on exactly the same fabric before you do the final stitching.

9. Place the darning foot on machine.

10. Place the fabric you want to *dribble* on in the embroidery hoop. Place the *right* side of the fabric down and have the *wrong* side of the fabric face up in the hoop.

Dribbling enhances many of our Fabriqué™ projects. It is generally the final treatment to stitch when embellishing your garment.

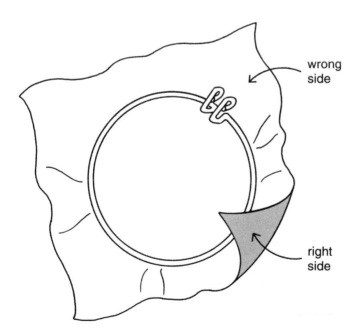

wrong side

right side

PRO QUOTE

When dribbling, the more erratic your wandering and stitch pattern is, the more visually interesting the dribbled clumps will be on the right side.

11. Lower (or lower to half position — depending on the brand of machine) the presser foot.

12. Take one stitch and pull the bobbin thread or yarn up to the top (wrong) side, just as in freehand embroidery. If the yarn is too thick to be pulled up to the top, hold it away with your left hand and away from the direction you are sewing. This will prevent you from accidentally stitching over it, which would produce a messy finish on the right side.

13. Hold both the bobbin and upper threads in your left hand until you've stitched the first few stitches. (If you don't do this, the threads can tangle and create a mess.) Then you can let go of them.

14. Now just stitch and wander randomly over the fabric surface. The wobblier you sew, the more interesting the final dribbles.

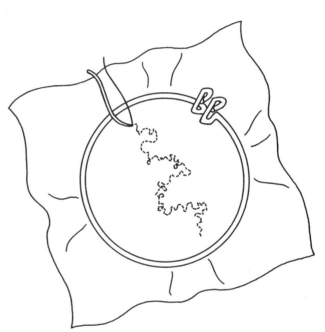

If the stitches are close together, the more the clumps on the right side will be knobbly. You can wander like a drunken sailor and stagger in the same place for a couple of stitches.

Pro Quote

Always use a water–soluble or disappearing marking pen when transferring stitching lines to the right side of the fabric. If your trims don't always cover up the marks, the stitching lines will be much easier to remove.

Generally speaking, the more erratic the stitches, the more interesting the texture will be on the right side surface.

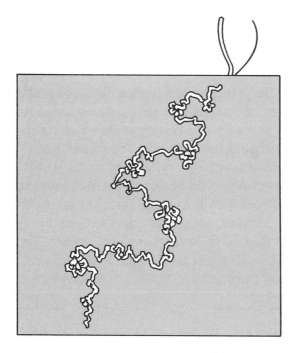

I recommend doing a couple of experimental samples. Use different yarns or threads on the bobbin. Wind the bobbin by machine and by hand and try samples of each method. Stitch erratically and wobbly. Then stitch straighter. Observe the differences and decide on the effect you want to create.

PRO QUOTE

When sewing repetitive lines of stitching, some "fabric shrinkage" will occur. Cut the pattern 1" bigger all the way around to allow for this.

Examples of dribbling. Heavier threads and yarns are wound on the bobbin; however, the yarn or thread does not pass through the bobbin tension gauge. It employs freehand stitching with the feed dog lowered or covered.

Matador Jacket

Couching, Cable Stitching, and Dribbling

Cable Stitching and couching are the primary techniques stitched on Margaret's red matador jacket. The background fabric is douppioni silk. Gold and black threads, gold cord, and black and gold braid are stitched or couched onto the fabric.

Notice the stitching begins at a higher area and gradually slopes down, wrapping the body in similar yet not quite parallel lines. The heavy black thread is applied by cable stitching (black thread on the bobbin and gold thread on the top of the machine). The gold metallic thread is applied by regular straight stitching. The gold cord and black and gold braid is couched onto the surface. Black rayon and gold metallic thread form the satin stitched lines. Also, a few of the lines are stitched using a dense decorative stitch and black rayon thread. In some of the areas where "open space" has been formed, a cluster of gold sequins is stitched in place by hand. Also notice, the stitching on the sleeves repeats the stitched design on the jacket.

Since some "fabric shrinkage" will occur when cable stitching and couching, add at least 1" (2.5 cm) around the entire cutting line of the pattern. Cut out the enlarged pattern, do all the decorative stitching, then recut the embellished fabric to your actual pattern size.

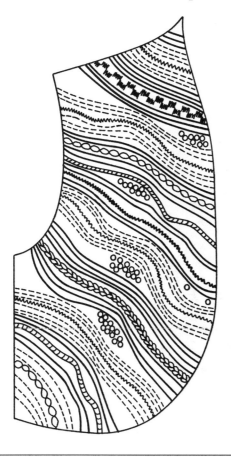

This particular jacket pattern features a side seam bust-fitting dart. It is stitched in place *after* all the decorative stitching is completed. The dart simply tends to get lost in the repetitive stitching lines. The sleeves feature similar repetitive stitching. The jacket is completely lined.

Stitching Key

—————————————	black cable stitch
- - - - - - - - - - -	gold straight stitch
wwwwwwwwwww	gold satin stitch
⨍⨍⨍⨍⨍⨍⨍⨍	decorative stitch pattern (1)
oᏰᎱ Ꭷₒₒᵒ ᎧᏰ ᎧᎧᏰₒ	sequins
∞∞∞∞∞∞∞∞∞	decorative stitch pattern (2)
⟋⟋⟋⟋⟋⟋⟋⟋⟋	gold cord couching
∿∿∿∿∿∿∿∿∿	black satin stitch
⋙⋙⋙⋙⋙⋙⋙	black and gold flat braid

Glenda's comfortable Italian wool jacket uses the techniques of scrunching, decorative machine embroidery, appliqué, satin stitching, and couching for this Fabriqué™ project.

Margaret's mauve blouse as viewed from the back. See Chapter 4 Appliqué: The Basics.

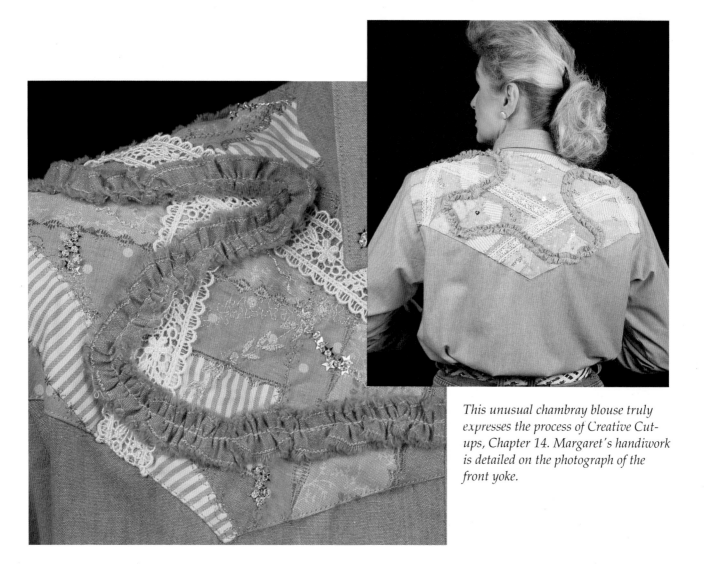

This unusual chambray blouse truly expresses the process of Creative Cut-ups, Chapter 14. Margaret's handiwork is detailed on the photograph of the front yoke.

This spectacular trio of blouses incorporate many Fabriqué™ ideas and techniques. Beginning from left to right, you'll see the turquoise chiffon blouse featuring Fabriqué™ Mélange (Chapter 11); the mauve polyester blouse with abstract appliqué shapes (Chapter 4); and the green sueded–silk blouse embellished with hand twisted scrunched appliqué (Chapter 7).

This comfortable outfit, designed by Margaret Lawtie, combines navy and red cotton and is embellished with appliqué and decorative gold stitching. A variation of this blouse is featured in the Project Page for Chapter 6, Puckering with Scribble Stitches.

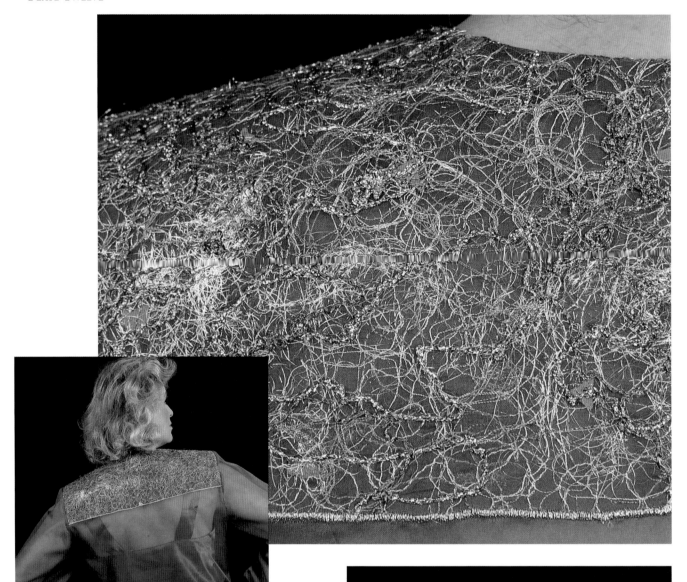

Chapter 11, Fabriqué™ Mélange, explains the easy steps to follow when creating mélange. Jenny has stitched this stunningly beautiful work of the mélange, which I then designed into yokes and cuffs on this elegant organza blouse.

Jenny's creativity is expressed beautifully in this green sueded–silk blouse. The bodice yokes and belt buckle uses mainly scrunching, dribbling, and satin-stitch bursts to embellish the outfit. Look at the close-up for details of the back yoke.

This dramatic red skirt and blouse was designed and sewn by Jenny Anastas. The yokes and coordinating belt buckle mainly feature scrunching, freehand stitching, dribbling, and satin-stitch bursts.

Jenny's effort, time, and creative skills really paid off when she won 1st prize in an Australian and New Zealand competition for creative machine embroidery with this douppioni silk outfit. This is truly a stunning wardrobe addition.

Creativity and self-expression come alive as shown here in these spectacular silk jackets. The models are truly "wrapped" in Fabriqué™!

Jenny's black mandarin jacket features freehand stitching done with gold metallic thread.

CHAPTER THIRTEEN

TUBES 'N TUNNELS

Tubes 'n tunnels is an easy technique that adds depth to fabric while providing an exciting flowing form of varying width and length. This chapter opens great possibilities with the fabric tubes by showing you ideas that use the tubes stitched together, separate, curved, and formed into various shapes. Depending on how closely they are stitched together, the space in between them can form a tunnel effect. This is a relatively easy process because these are unturned tubes. Actually, you will be creating padded bias fabric strips and stitching over the outer raw edge to secure them to the background fabric. The tubes can also be rolled into spiral shapes which are hand stitched onto the final project.

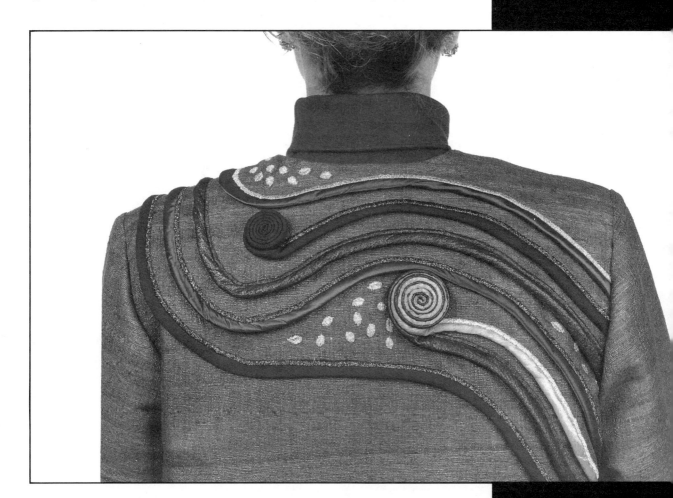

SUGGESTED APPLICATION AND USAGE

Because this procedure creates a relatively heavy look, I have applied the tubes onto a raw silk jacket. Depending on the fabric choice for the padded tubes, you may consider stitching them onto a vest or coat.

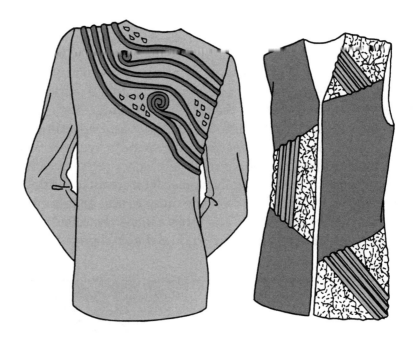

Another possible option is to create shapes for wall hangings or other home deco projects. An interesting option is to apply Tubes 'n Tunnels to the surface of a quilt, coordinating colors with those of the room.

I suggest reading through this process and doing a test sample before beginning an actual project.

SPECIFIC MATERIALS AND SUPPLIES

• Fabric for tubes
• Fabric for background
• Thread (general sewing and specialty threads)
• Metalfil or embroidery needle
• Fusible fleece
• Iron–on interfacing or fusible, tear–away stabilizer
• Tracing vellum
• Disappearing fabric-marking pencil or dressmaker's carbon and tracing wheel
• Rotary cutter and mat
• Appliqué mat (optional)

Preparing the Pattern

1. Decide on the garment pattern you would like to embellish with Tubes 'n Tunnels (vest, coat, or jacket).

2. Decide on the section of the pattern to be embellished. Copy a pattern of this section on tracing vellum.

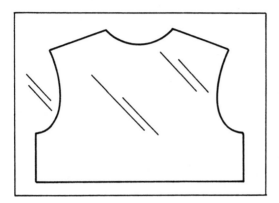

3. Decide on the design, shape, and movement the tubes are to follow by sketching on the tracing vellum. When deciding on the flow of the tubes, also decide where the tube will end. It can be carried off into a seam allowance and thereby sandwiched in the ensuing seam. It could also just stop and then you could cover the raw edge with further embellishment such as a scrunched appliqué.

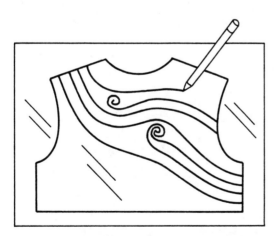

4. Measure the length of each placement area so that you will know how long to cut each fabric strip. Make sure to allow sufficient length on any tubes that will end in a spiral shape.

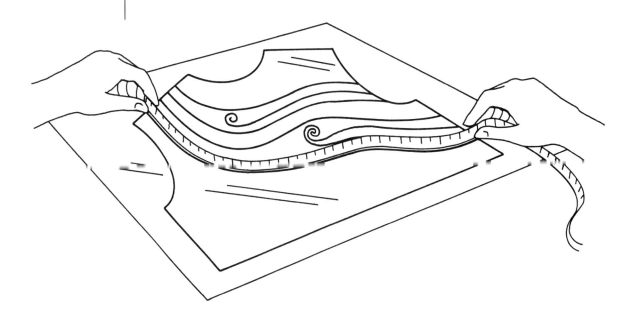

Preparing the Background Fabric

The pattern section that you wish to embellish can be treated in one of two ways.

Option 1: The tubes can be sewn directly onto the garment thereby making the garment the background fabric.

Pro Quote

Bondable fleece makes creating padded tubes a breeze.

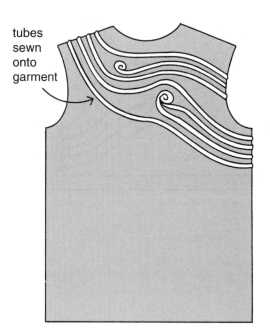

tubes sewn onto garment

Option 2: The section to be embellished could be cut as an overlaying yoke piece that would lie on top of the garment and be stitched into appropriate seams. It would have an appropriate finish, like a satin stitch applied to the loose edge. The yoke then becomes the background fabric.

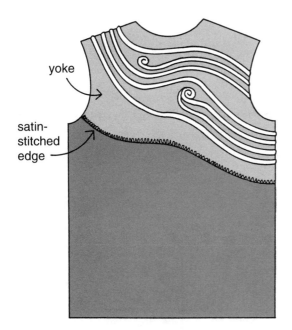

When choosing one of the above methods, make sure to calculate additional fabric to prepare the yokes or overlays described in option #2.

Stabilize the Background Fabric

Whichever of the above options you choose, you will need to stabilize the background area where you will apply the tubes.

- Experiment with applying iron–on interfacing (this would then become a permanent feature of the garment).

- Another option is to back the area with tear–away stabilizer. I prefer the bondable tear–away (Totally Stable, for example). If you use the nonfusible type (Stitch and Tear), it would be best to baste the stabilizer in place before beginning tube application.

PRO QUOTE

Using a bondable, tear–away stabilizer makes stabilizing the background fabric a very easy process. All can be torn away after stitching is completed, except for the little bit caught in the stitches.

Strip Preparation

1. Choose compatible colors with the background fabric to form the tubes. Monochromatic color choices work well and create a subtle finished effect. Contrasting colors will create a more showy piece.

2. Choose relatively soft fabrics that have flexibility. The stiffer the fabric, the less easily the tubes will bend to create your design.

3. Using a rotary cutter and cutting mat, cut the fabric into 2 ¹⁄₂" (6.4 cm) wide true bias strips. The length of the strip is determined by the distance or length of the tube's placement area.

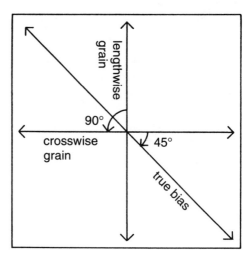

4. Cut strips of fusible fleece 1" (2.5 cm) wide. The same length of fleece is needed to match the length of the fabric strips.

5. Lay the bondable side of the fusible fleece down the center of the wrong side of the bias strip.

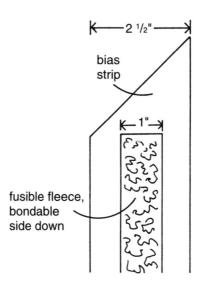

6. Place an appliqué mat or piece of tracing vellum over the top and press, thereby fusing the fleece to the fabric strip.

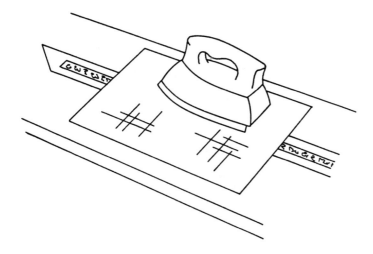

7. Fold the padded strip in half, wrong sides together, thereby enclosing the fleece. Using a thread color that is compatible with the color of the tube fabric, straight stitch raw edges together with a $5/8$" (1.6 cm) seam allowance.

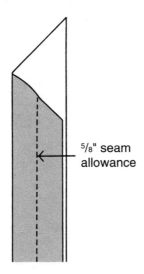

$5/8$" seam allowance

8. Trim away excess seam allowance to within $1/16$" (2 mm) of the stitching.

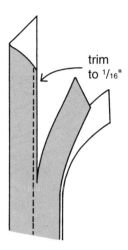

trim
to $1/16$"

Glenda's brown wool vest, shown on color plate #7, uses a combination of scrunched copper-colored lamé, linen torn strips, and complementary tubes 'n tunnels. This shoulder close-up shows you the creative detail.

Application of the Tube

1. Transfer the desired design onto the stabilized background fabric where the tubes are to be placed. This can be done with a fabric-marking pencil or with dressmaker's carbon and tracing wheel.

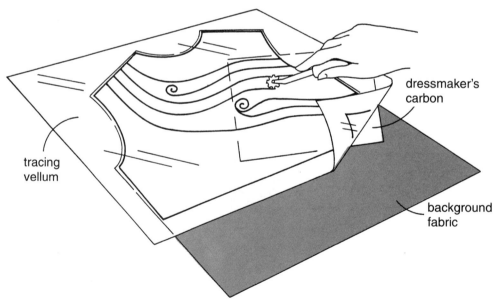

dressmaker's carbon

tracing vellum

background fabric

2. Always begin on the left-hand side of the design and repeat each step of this application process for each tube, before applying subsequent tubes.

3. Lay the tube along the positioning placement line on the background fabric. Pin randomly.

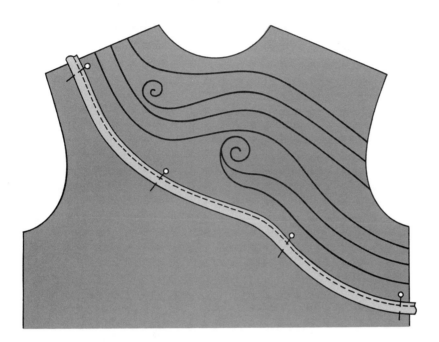

4. Straight stitch through the first set of stitches, thereby securing the tube to the background fabric. You may need to change the sewing machine's foot to one that will ride comfortably on the raised bulk of the tube and that has a good sized channel on the underside of the foot.

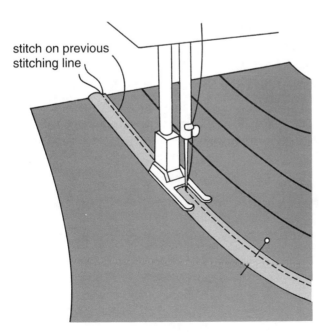

stitch on previous stitching line

130

5. Choose a color of rayon or metallic thread that either blends, complements, or contrast the color of the tube and background fabric.

6. Put a metalfil or embroidery needle on the machine.

7. Set the machine for satin stitch zigzag. Stitch over top of the previous stitching so that the satin stitch completely covers the original straight stitch and the raw edge.

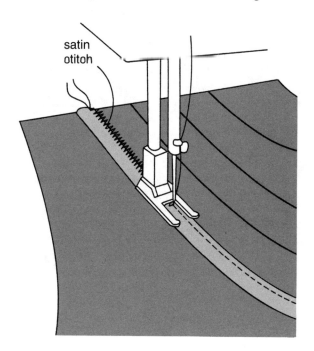

satin
otitoh

PRO QUOTE

When using cable stitching for the final trim, the previous line of straight stitches guide when stitching from the wrong side.

8. You may want to sew this decorative stitch step with a heavier thread or yarn. Therefore, satin stitching with a cable stitch is an option. (Heavier yarn is wound on the bobbin. Bobbin tension is loosened. Stitching is done with right side of fabric facing downward, wrong side of fabric is up.) See Chapter 12 on Couching, Cable Stitching, and Dribbling.

9. Now, repeat the above steps of the application process with each and every tube, working from left to right.

Finishing Details for Tubes

• Enclose ends in subsequent seams during garment construction.

- If the tubes do not end in a seam allowance, cover exposed tube ends with scrunched appliqué, manipulated torn strips, or tube spirals.

- Try experimenting with constructing wider and narrower tubes. Place these graded sizes of tubes in parallel lines. Also try wobbling the position of the tubes and creating irregular rhythm and movement.

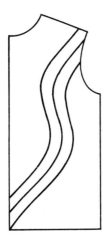

- In addition to the tubes, try enhancing the final project with couching, thread wrapping, or dribbling on the background fabric.

Spiral Tube Design

1. Prepare the padded tube up to enclosing the fusible fleece in the first line of stitching. (Steps 1–7, Strip Preparation)

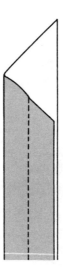

A beautiful asymmetrical design is created when I continued the tube detailing only over the left shoulder. Spiral tubes with long tails complete the shoulder accent.

2. Trim seam allowance to $1/8$" (.3 cm).

3. Zigzag over raw edge. This helps prevent fraying while forming the spiral shape.

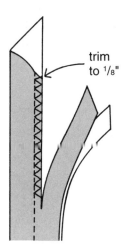

trim to $1/8$"

4. Tuck the raw end down so that it won't show, and begin rolling the tube in a tight spiral form.

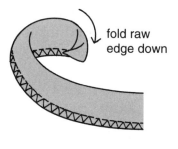

fold raw edge down

5. As you roll, you will need to hand stitch the zigzagged edges together, thereby securing the spiral shape.

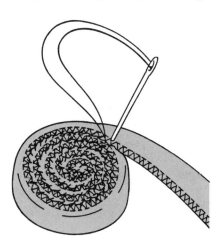

6. The spiral shape can be made as large as you want.

7. The final end can be tucked underneath, or the raw edges could be tucked inside the tube and then stitched to the outer edge of the shape.

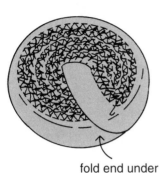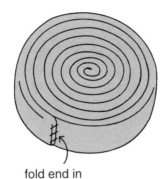

fold end under   fold end in

8. Position the formed spiral onto the background fabric. Hand stitch it in place.

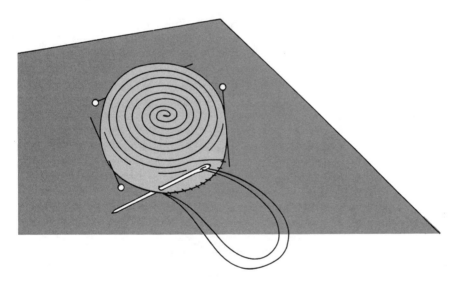

Spiral Tubes with Two Contrasting Colors

1. Prepare the padded tubes so that the fleece is enclosed in the first line of stitching, (steps 1–7, Strip Preparation).

2. Lay the tubes one on top of the other and stitch them together on top of the previous stitching line.

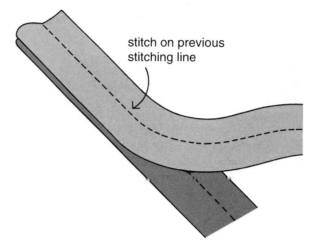

stitch on previous
stitching line

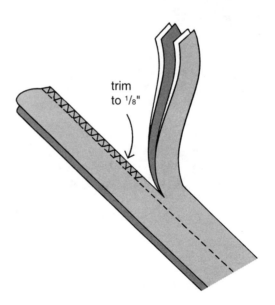
3. Trim seam allowance to within $1/8$" (.3 cm) of the stitching.

4. Zigzag stitch over the trimmed edge, which will help prevent fraying when forming the spiral shape.

trim
to $1/8$"

5. Begin rolling and hand stitching the two tubes together to form the spiral shape. Make the shape as large as you wish.

6. Finish ends.

7. Hand stitch to background fabric.

Spiral Tubes with Long, Flowing Ends

1. Prepare enough padded tubing to form a continuous spiral. Allow enough length for the "tail" to come off the spiral and be stitched onto the background fabric.

2. Decide how much of the tube will form the spiral and how much will be the tail.

3. For each tube, do all padding, folding, and stitching. Trim the section that will form the spiral to $1/8$" (.3 cm) and the remainder of the tube to $1/16$" (2 mm). Next, zigzag stitch over the trimmed edge only on the section that will form the continuous spiral.

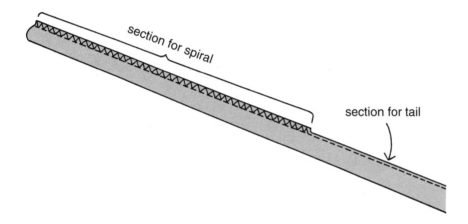

section for spiral

section for tail

4. Roll and hand stitch the continuous spiral shape up to where the zigzag ends.

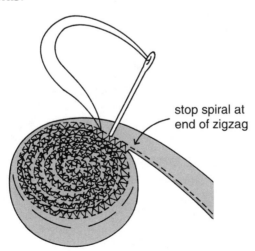

stop spiral at end of zigzag

5. Position this spiral with tails on the background fabric. Straight stitch the tail by machine onto the background fabric.

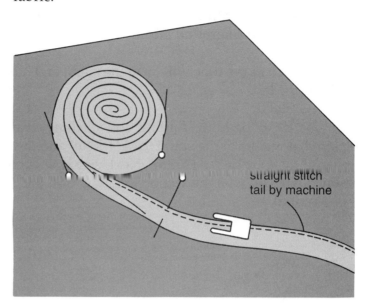

6. Satin stitch the tail to the background fabric covering the raw edge and the previous line of stitching and ending as close to the spiral as possible.

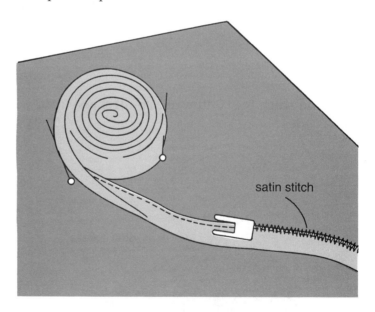

7. Hand stitch the spiral shape onto the background fabric.
    Make sure the spiral is placed to cover any raw edges not
    covered with satin stitching.

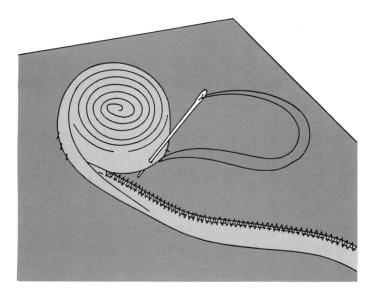

Experiment with variations of the above spiral shapes. Try
making the padded tubes smaller or larger. Try forming the shape
into an oval rather than a circle. Try wrapping two different colors
of tubes together and leaving long tails that become an integral
part of the design. Experiment and enjoy your creativity.

![Tubes 'n Tunnels Vest]

Tubes 'n Tunnels Vest

Tubes 'n Tunnels

This chapter's highlight is a worsted wool vest that features geometric panels containing Tubes 'n Tunnels, scrunched fabric, and torn strips.

Use any similar style vest pattern (mine uses Sure–Fit Designs™). Draw the paneled areas and add 1" (2.5 cm) of extra cutting room around all edges.

The copper-colored lamé is scrunched by hand twisting. The tubes are formed and stitched following the directions in this chapter. I have sewn most of the tubes from a coarse linen. Two are sewn from copper lamé. The torn strips are prepared from the same linen. Each torn strip edge is satin stitched. A basting stitch is sewn down the center of the strip and gently gathered before stitching onto the designated area. The gold netting was scrunched by Method 4, as described in Chapter 7.

The large pieces of scrunched lamé are appliquéd to the fabric first. Space for the tubes is then determined and left open. Next, stitch the gold netting in place. Small pieces of scrunched lamé are then appliquéd in place. The torn strip is then laid inplace and meanders its way across the panel. Next, the fabric tubes are stitched in place. Recut the embellished panels by the correct pattern shapes.

These embellished panels are then sewn to the front vest sections. Because some of the tubes will be stitched across and turned to the inside as the lining is sewn in place, remove some of the bulk of the tube. *Carefully* fold back the tube fabric and, with sharp pointed embroidery scissors, remove some of the fleece. Lay the outer tube fabric back in place. The raw edge of each panel is first stitched with straight stitching, then decoratively cable stitched with a wide stitch pattern. The remainder of the armscye, side seam, center front, and hem line seams are enclosed as the lining is applied.

Right Front Embellished Panel

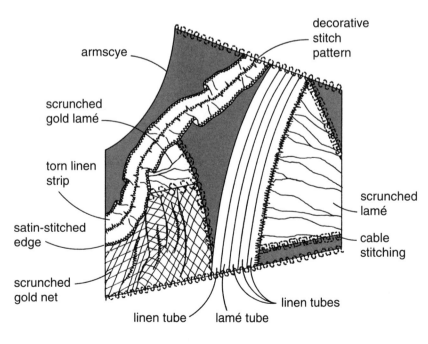

armscye

decorative stitch pattern

scrunched gold lamé

torn linen strip

satin-stitched edge

scrunched gold net

scrunched lamé

cable stitching

linen tubes

linen tube   lamé tube

CHAPTER FOURTEEN

CREATIVE CUT–UPS

CREATIVE CUT–UPS literally take different colors, patterns, and fabric textures, cuts them all up in strips, and then sews them back together again by mixing up the various colors and patterns. The recreated fabric is then further cut into sections, mixed up some more, and then randomly sewn back together again. The result is exciting, unique, and can be further influenced by the fabrics initially selected and by any further embellishment you may wish to add.

140

SUGGESTED
APPLICATION
AND USAGE

Once your cutting–up and reconstruction sewing is complete, you can use the final piece to make accessories like clutch purses, eyeglasses cases, or even as "fabric" to cut out yokes, pockets, and cuffs.

If you use the recreated fabric for yokes, pockets, or cuffs of a garment, make sure you buy enough fabric for the main body of the garment plus at least 12" (30 cm) more so that it can be used as one of the four fabrics required in the final recreated fabric.

PRO QUOTE

A rotary cutting wheel and accompanying cutting mat are useful tools to use for many different projects where cutting straight lines are essential.

SPECIFIC
MATERIALS
AND SUPPLIES

- Fabric (at least four different, compatible colors, or patterns)
- Thread (general sewing and specialty threads)
- Heavier textured threads (optional)
- Lace (optional)
- Sequins or beads (optional)
- Twin (double) needle (optional)
- Rotary cutter and cutting mat
- Tear–away stabilizer
- Embroidery hoop

1. Choose at least four different yet coordinating fabrics. The pieces should be about 12" (30 cm) x 45" (115 cm). The chambray blouse uses a solid light blue colored chambray for the body of the blouse. Three chambray prints coordinate with the main fabric.

2. Cut from selvage to selvage, strips of fabric that are 2" (5.1 cm) wide using a rotary cutter and cutting mat. If your fabric is 45" (115 cm) wide, the strips of fabric will be this length. Do this to all four pieces of fabric, thereby giving you six strips of each fabric piece.

METHOD

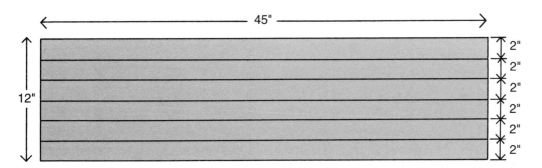

3. With the long edges of the fabric together, lay the strips of fabric side by side. In doing so, alternate the plain color with the various patterned fabric. With fabric right sides together, straight stitch the long strips together with ¹/₄" (.6 cm) seam allowance.

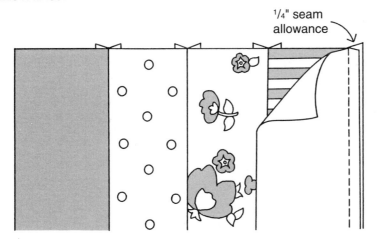

Continue this process of alternating strips and stitching them together until all strips are sewn together.

4. Press all ¹/₄" (.6 cm) seams open.

PRO QUOTE

One great aspect about creative cut–ups is that you can use any number of different colors of similar textured fabric. Any combination will be suitable.

5. Begin embellishing each seam. Choose various decorative sewing machine stitch patterns. Choose various, yet coordinating colors of metallic and rayon thread. You may choose to use a twin (double) needle and two different yet coordinating or contrasting colors of top thread. You may need to stabilize the fabric by backing with a tear–away stabilizer or placing fabric taut inside the embroidery hoop. Try a few test stitches and threads. Then begin to stitch on top of each previously sewn seam with your chosen stitch patterns and thread colors.

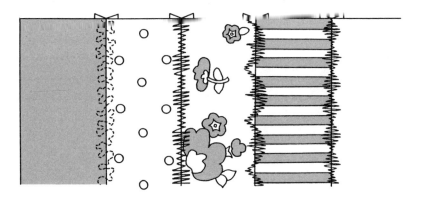

6. This next step is best done with a rotary cutter and cutting mat. Take this recreated and embellished fabric and further cut it into irregular and odd-shaped pieces. These cuts can be random and done wherever you feel like making them. Think of this as creating an easy jigsaw puzzle. You are creating the puzzle pieces.

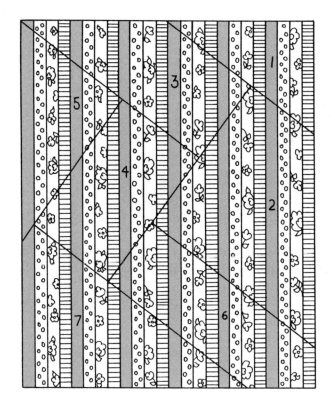

PRO QUOTE

Cutting the stitched strips of fabric into random shapes and repositioning the seams may seem challenging. However, because cuts are random, the restitched seams are also completely random. You can not make any mistakes.

Next you are going to take all the puzzle's pieces and turn them at different angles so that none of the original stripes match up. You are taking a cut–up shape and matching its cut edge with a totally different edge and angle of another cut–up shape. You might like to match two sets of strips to form a chevron effect. Or you can randomly place the cut edge of one shape to the cut edge of another shape. Once again, seam these cut edges by placing right sides together and stitching with a straight stitch and $1/4$" (.6 cm) seam allowances.

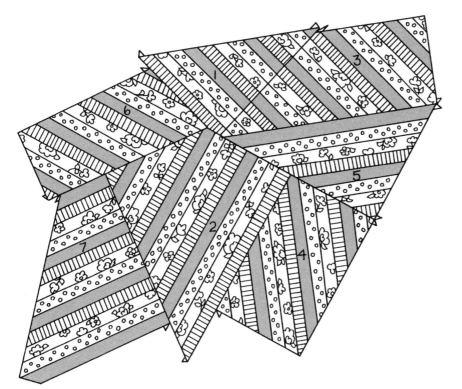

The cutting-up and creative stitching process is shown here before any further decorative embellishment is added.

During this cutting and rejoining process you will likely create some sharp points and angles that get in the way when you're sewing the cut–up shapes back together. Cut these unnecessary points off.

7.   Press these newly created seams open.

144

8. Now, decorate and embellish these seams with more decorative machine embroidery stitches. You will find that these seams tend to be more bulky; therefore, you may want to use machine stitch patterns that are more open (rather than the tighter, closed satin stitches).

PRO QUOTE

The more cuts you make, the more seams you will have to rejoin back together. And that's great because you'll end up with more interesting intersections when you lay the pattern pieces down to be cut out.

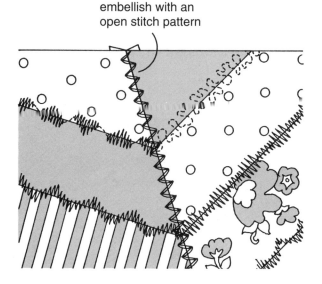

embellish with an open stitch pattern

9. Your creative cut–up fabric is now ready for you to cut out the yoke, pocket, and/or cuff pattern pieces. Because it is impossible to take into account the grainline direction, pattern pieces should be laid where there is a visually interesting intersection of strips and stitching.

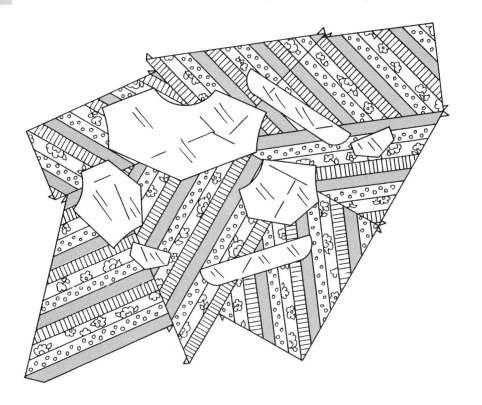

10. If putting a yoke in both front and back of the garment, pin yokes together at shoulder seam, stitch with ⁵/₈" (1.6 cm) seam allowance, then press open. Next sew a decorative embroidery stitch to top stitch this shoulder seam.

You have now completed the process of creative cut–ups. You can now construct the remainder of the garment following pattern instructions; however, you may wish to further embellish your creative cut–up fabric before constructing the garment. The chambray blouse shown in this chapter was further embellished with the following techniques.

*   A variety of decorative embroidery stitches can be added anywhere you want. Back the yoke with a tear–away stabilizer or use the embroidery hoop where you plan to add the decorative stitches. Stitch, then tear the backing away. For the chambray blouse, we have selected a silver metallic thread and a couple of floral type machine stitches and then simply *wandered* over the yoke pattern pieces.

*   Next, if you wish to add any dribbling do so at this time. See Chapter 12 on Dribbling. The dribbling on the chambray shirt was done with a silver metallic thread wound on the bobbin. Meander the dribbling in any direction you choose.

*   If you wish to add complimentary lace, do so at this time.

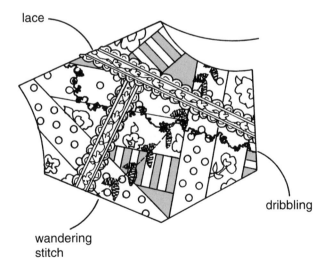

lace

dribbling

wandering stitch

• You may also continue embellishing the creative cut–up fabric with sequins and beads or by adding some torn strips. Both of these options were added to the chambray blouse. For preparation of the torn strips, see Chapter 8 on Fabric Strip Manipulation. With this example, narrow 1" (2.5 cm) chambray strips were stitched 1/4" (.6 cm) away from the raw edge and then fringed up to the stitching line. A long gathering stitch was sewn down the center of the strip. The chambray strip was then lightly gathered and randomly laid onto the surface of the creative cut–up fabric. Then it was straight stitched down the center to attach it to the surface of the cut–up fabric.

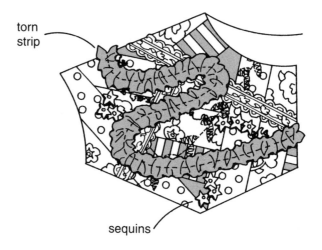

• Once all of the surface embellishment has been completed on the creative cut–up fabric, begin constructing the garment following pattern directions — or proceed in your preferred manner of construction.

Margaret used her creative cut-up fabric to cut yokes and cuffs for this casual blouse. Further embellishment in the form of Fabriqué™ torn strips and dribbling and decorative stitches, lace, and sequins application complete her creative garment.

Creative Cut–Ups

If you like the blue chambray blouse, the main yoke and cuff treatment is cut from prepared creative cut–ups. As you follow the step–by–step procedures in this chapter, you will be able to produce a result similar to this example.

Blue chambray cotton is the chosen background fabric. Three additional chambray prints are used to create the cut–up fabric.

The pattern is drawn from the Sure–Fit Designs™ Shirt Kit. The yoke is drawn with points giving it a slight western rendition.

Silver metallic thread is the dominant color choice to compliment the blue chambray; however, blue and green metallic and rayon threads are also used to stitch together the cut–up strips. Silver dribbling, done with metallic yarn, also enhances the cut–up creation.

Torn strips of chambray with raw fringed edges add further embellishment to the creative cut–up yokes and cuffs. See Chapter 8 for details on creating stunning fabric strips. Purchased lace is also stitched to the yokes and cuffs in a wandering pattern.

Finally, complimentary silver buttons complete this comfortable shirt.

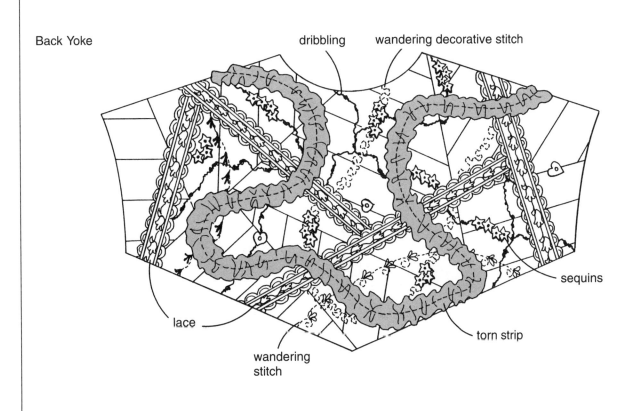

Back Yoke — dribbling — wandering decorative stitch — sequins — torn strip — lace — wandering stitch

PERSONAL
NOTES

CHAPTER FIFTEEN

FROM START TO FINISH

–

A PROJECT IN DETAIL

T HE TECHNIQUES OF FABRIQUÉ™ expand your abilities to manipulate any piece of fabric you want, embellish any garment you want, and create any design you can imagine. The beauty of Fabriqué™ is that you are free to do what you want. Your final result will be special and stunning. Remember, you can make *no* mistakes.

For this vest project, I have segmented every step in the process up to final construction. You will discover the true joy and ease of using Fabriqué™ techniques to achieve that singular garment of unmatched beauty. Join with me in this experience of gratification when your finished Fabriqué™ garment stands out — the compliments you receive make the effort worthy of your time. As you work through and understand this process you will be able to apply similar project steps to any embellished garment you wish to make.

METHOD

1. Decide on the garment to be embellished. I have chosen a vest. This vest has been designed from the Sure-Fit Designs™ Shirt Kit. Draw the pattern with tracing vellum. Draw a complete right- and left-side back pattern. Draw right- and left- side front patterns.

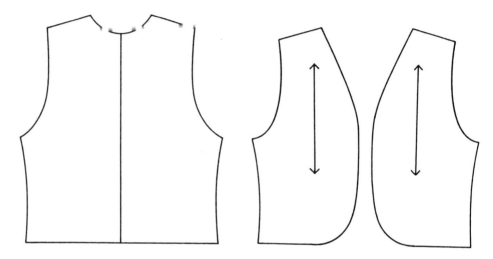

PRO QUOTE

Accomplishing this project will give you skills that are generally transferable to any Fabriqué™ project.

2. Have a piece of backing fabric available. Plain-colored lining, cotton, cotton–poly blend or 100% polyester is generally suitable. This should be cut larger by at least 2–3" (2.5–7.6 cm) around all edges of the pattern pieces. With tailor's chalk or soap, draw an outline of the pattern piece on backing fabric.

2"–3" extra fabric

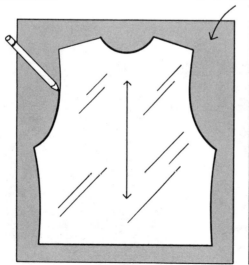
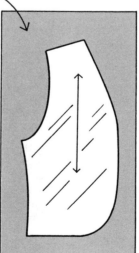
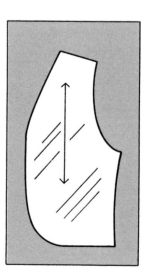

3. Decide on and draw the shapes and sizes of the fabric pieces that you would like to appliqué onto the front and back of the vest. These can be free-flowing curves or angular, geometric shapes. When drawing Step 3 on the front pattern pieces, you will probably not want a mirror image from one side to the other. Draw compatible yet different appliqué shapes on both sides.

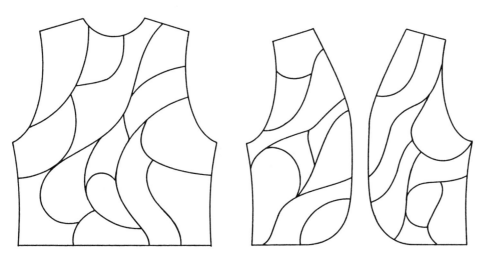

Free-flowing curves

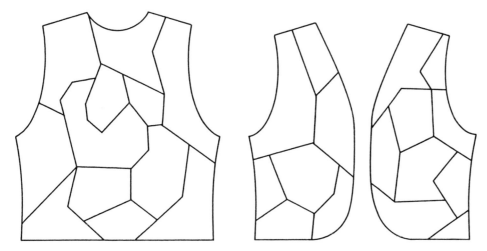

Random geometric shapes

4. Collect all the different colors and textures of fabrics that you would like to use on the project. Colors should be compatible. Fabrics should have similarities in both thickness and weight.

5. Collect all the different threads, yarns, and trims that you think you would like to use.

6. Think about the location of where you want different fabrics to be placed on the final garment. Before manipulating the fabrics, lay them side by side to make sure you like the look.

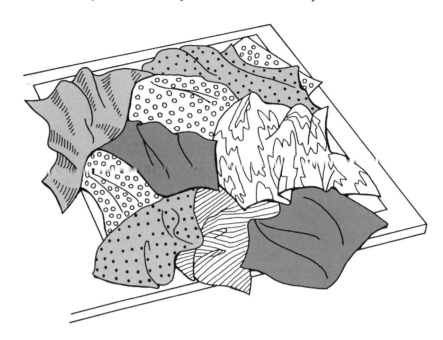

7. Begin manipulating chosen pieces of fabric by your selected techniques. For example, see the accompanying schematic for the techniques used on this sample vest.

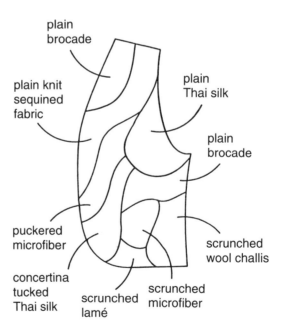

8. Prepare/sew all fabrics that you want manipulated (for example, scrunch, pin tuck, and/or pucker selected fabric pieces as desired).

9. Number all the pattern segments as shown. For example, use "B–1" to indicate "back 1," use RF–2 to indicate "right front 2," use "LF–1" to indicate left front 1, and so on.

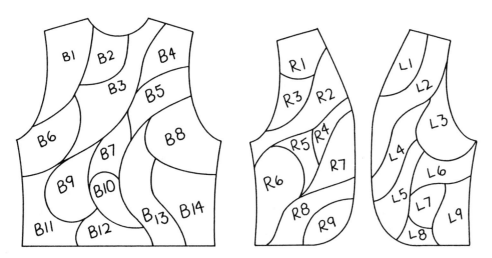

10. Turn the pattern over so that the wrong side is up. Lay paper–backed, fusible webbing over the pattern. Make certain that the fusible side of the webbing is face down on the wrong side of the pattern. The paper side is face up so that you can copy the appliqué shape on the paper.

11. Draw the individual pattern appliqué shapes on the paper–backed fusible webbing, leaving an allowance of about $^3/_8$" (1.0 cm) on all edges. When you draw edges where there will be a seam (at the shoulder seam, for example) leave at least $^5/_8$" (1.6 cm) *extra* allowance.

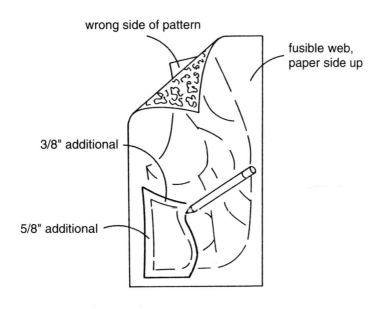

12. Label all appliqué pieces on the paper–backed fusible webbing with the corresponding number of the pattern piece ("B–1," "B–2," "B–3," etc.).

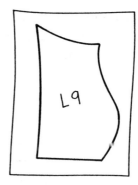

13. Cut out the paper–backed fusible appliqué shapes.

14. Following the manufacturer's directions, bond the fusible side of one appliqué shape to the *wrong* side of your selected manipulated fabric piece.

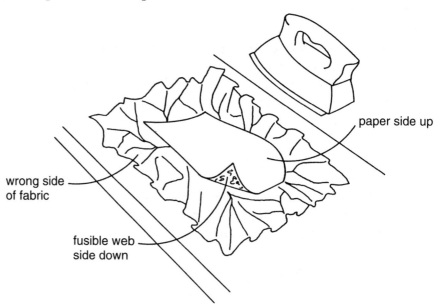

paper side up

wrong side
of fabric

fusible web
side down

15. Prepare and bond all remaining manipulated fabric pieces with paper–backed, fusible webbing. Complete this step for the entire front and back of vest.

16. Lay all bonded fabric pieces onto the backing fabric (lining or cotton material) and pin in place thereby *composing* the design as drawn on your initial vellum pattern. Just see how it looks and decide if you are satisfied with it at this stage.

This is the time to change any segments if you want a particular section of fabric manipulated in a different way or if you want different colors of fabric to be side by side. Trim all bonded fabric pieces to their cutting line. Decide which shapes will overlap and which edge will be on top. Remember that light colors should always go underneath the darker ones. Do any additional trimming if necessary.

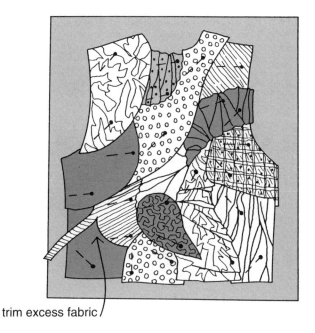

trim excess fabric

17. Once satisfied on your choices of color, shapes, and placements, begin removing the paper backing from the fusible webbing and fuse/bond the manipulated fabric pieces onto the base fabric. Lay your vest pattern piece on top to check that the pattern form you are creating follows your original outline.

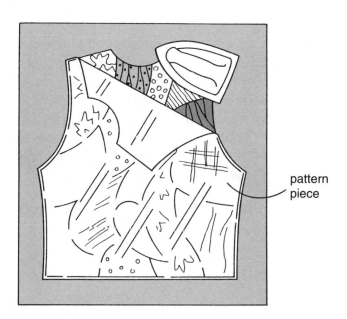

pattern piece

As shown on color plate #3, this vest, designed and sewn by Jenny, is a combination of geometric shapes and features many decorative stitch patterns.

156

18. When all fabric pieces are fused in place, and before you begin to stitch them permanently to the backing fabric, test different embroidery and decorative stitches and colors of thread you would like to use to sew the pieces in place.

I recommend taking the leftover scraps of prepared fabric and fusing them to any leftover backing fabric. Don't worry about shape and form, just fuse them down with similar colors contacting each other as they will be on the finished garment.

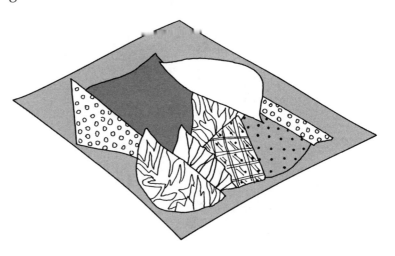

19. Place test fabric in embroidery hoop. Test sew stitches with various machine stitch patterns. Test stitch each pattern with various colors of threads. Decide on the embroidery stitch patterns you like and the colors of threads you like. Have a piece of paper and pen beside your sewing machine so that you can record the stitch patterns, lengths, widths, and choice of thread so that you don't have to try to remember those you liked.

When you are choosing your desired stitch patterns, choose patterns that are fairly dense so that when you stitch over the raw edges no future fraying will occur. If you want to use a freehand serpentine stitch, go over the raw edge at least four times. If you use a machine with a "cornelly"-type built–in stitch (see Chapter 2 Know the Terms), sewing over the edge only once should be sufficient. Decorative types of close satin stitches are also very appropriate to use.

Also try twin (double) needle stitching with different colors of thread and decorative satin stitches.

PRO QUOTE

When doing test samples of a particular stitch or manipulation process, always use the same fabric and threads that will go into the finished project.

20. Before you begin actually stitching the fabric pieces in place, decide where you should begin sewing. Whichever piece you stitch down first may ultimately be crossed over when you stitch another piece. Decide which one needs to be stitched in place first and which one you want to stitch last. The pieces that get stitched last will appear to be on top of the others.

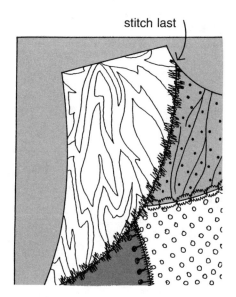

stitch last

PRO QUOTE

Keep a note pad and pen beside your sewing machine. As you test stitch, jot down the patterns you like and any special machine settings that would need repeating. Don't trust your memory.

21. Secure the area to be stitched tightly in the embroidery hoop. Begin sewing piece by piece and attach all fabric pieces with your chosen variety of decorative stitches and thread colors.

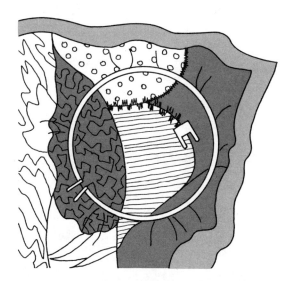

Just a note of caution: if you need to leave the project for any length of time, take the fabric out of the embroidery hoop so that the fabric grain won't stretch out of shape.

The following illustration is an example of what your vest might look like after all appliqué shapes have been sewn in place with decorative stitching.

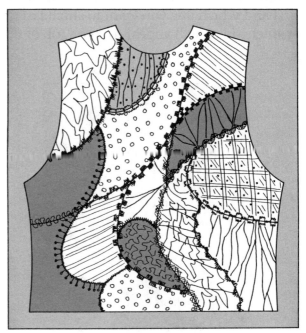

Decorative stitches attach all appliqué pieces.

22. After all pieces are sewn onto the backing fabric, decide if you want to sew any other decorative machine stitches throughout your creation. You can wander these stitch patterns randomly across the entire design, or intentionally keep them to one specific area.

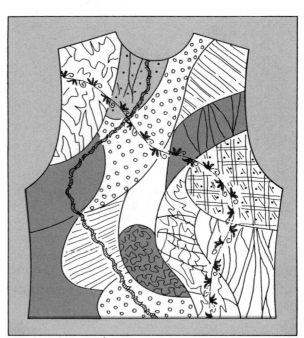

"Wandering" stitches add further embellishment.
(Previous stitching has been omitted for clarity.)

23. If you want to apply any couched trims or braids on the
surface, now is the time to do so.

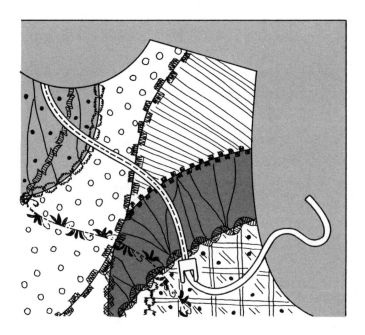

24. Last, but not least, "dribbling" can be done. See Chapter 12.
Because this is stitched from the wrong side of the fabric,
decide the approximate location of the stitched-on dribbles.
Hold the total piece in one hand, take your fabric-marking
pen, and randomly wander around the wrong side on the
backing fabric marking an approximate pattern where you
would like to stitch. Place fabric in your embroidery hoop
and begin dribbling.

Wind bobbin with heavy thread or decorative yarn such as
gold fingering. Place in bobbin case. Bypass bobbin thread
tension. Pull bobbin thread up. With fabric in the hoop, the
right *side* face down, and the feed dog not engaged, take one
stitch, thereby pulling bobbin thread up to the top side. Hold

both bobbin and top thread in left hand. Begin stitching along your random pattern. The more "wobbling" you do, the chunkier it will look on the right side. Have fun!

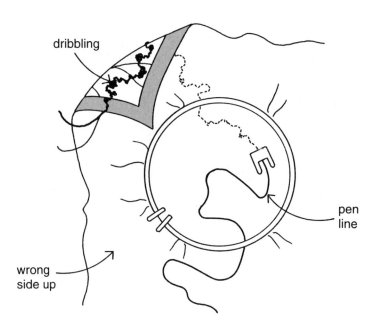

Glenda's vest features the application of many Fabriqué™ techniques such as scrunching, concertina tucking, puckering with scribble stitches, and dribbling to name a few. Look for the fuchsia–black–gold vest on color plate #3 for a vivid impression.

25. Trim away excess backing fabric using vest pattern pieces as your guideline. Sew garment together in usual construction method. This garment needs to be completely lined to cover all inside work.

CHAPTER SIXTEEN

USABLE PATTERNS, SHAPES, & MOTIFS

T HIS CHAPTER offers you additional patterns, shapes, and motifs. Use them in any manner you deem fit. They are here to stimulate your creativity and uniqueness, so change the patterns as you wish or use them as is.

SUGGESTED APPLICATION AND USAGE

The suggested shapes are intended to be appliquéd onto a backing or background fabric; however, before your chosen fabric is cut into the appliqué shape, I recommend that it first be manipulated using one of the Fabriqué™ techniques. Read on for a variety of ideas.

SPECIFIC MATERIALS AND SUPPLIES

- Tracing vellum
- Designing Stylus™ or french curve
- Designer's Companion
- T–square
- Yardstick or ruler
- Rotary cutter and cutting mat
- Paper scissors
- Teflon appliqué mat

METHOD

For the leaf shape, try creating a piece of Fabriqué™ Mélange. See Chapter 11. Then cut the leaf shape. The veins of the leaf could be added by satin stitching.

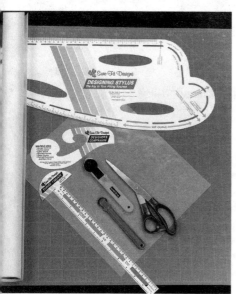

This is a display of some of the handy tools you should consider having available in your sewing room or area. Rotary cutter and mat, tracing wheel, designing tools, paper scissors, and tracing vellum to name a few.

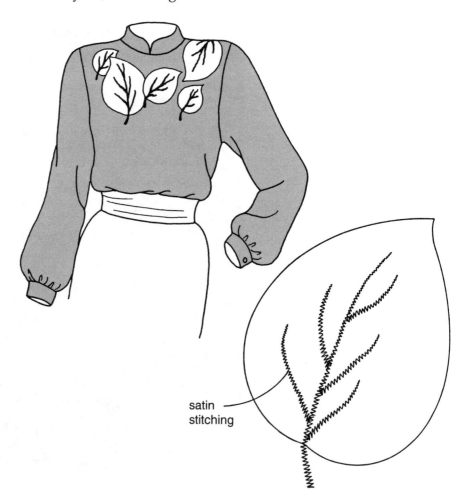

satin stitching

For the paisley shape, try scrunching by hand twisting the fabric. With a smaller inset paisley, try scrunching by manually pushing the fabric under the presser foot.

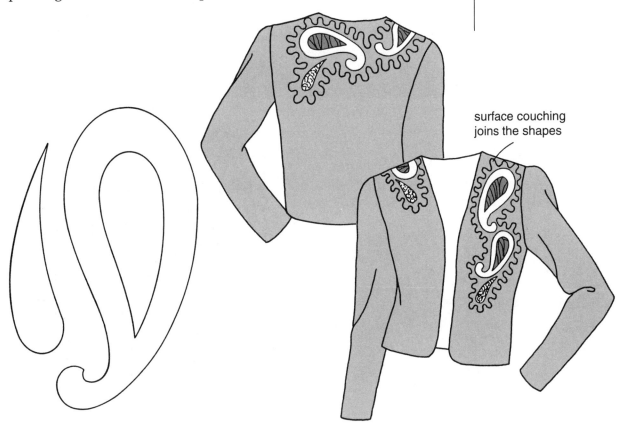

surface couching
joins the shapes

For the shell shapes, try pin-tucking the fabric.

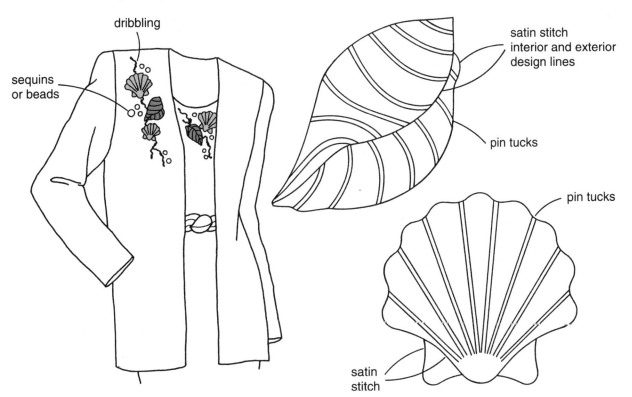

dribbling

sequins
or beads

satin stitch
interior and exterior
design lines

pin tucks

pin tucks

satin
stitch

For the elongated shapes, you may want to use nonmanipulated fabric, but then surround the shape with row upon row of freehand stitching as Jenny did on her douppioni silk jacket. Or, you could lay in a center elongated shape that has been scrunched, then sewn to the larger background shape.

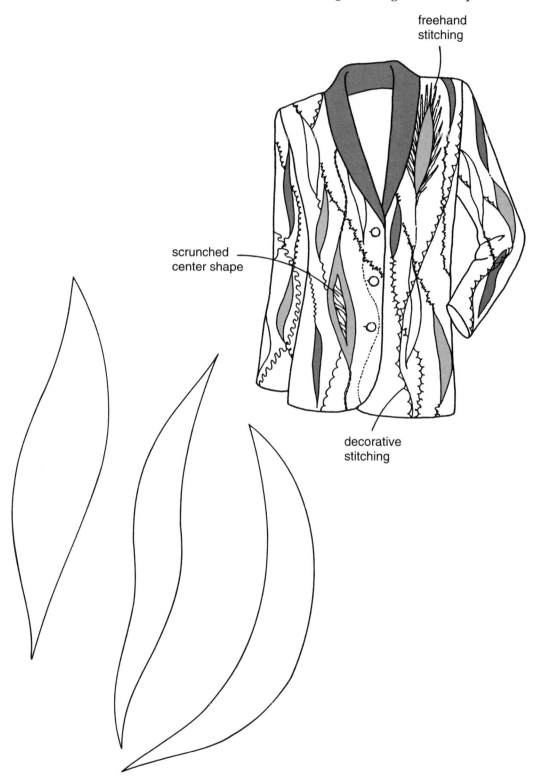

freehand stitching

scrunched center shape

decorative stitching

For the basic square, rectangle, or triangle shapes, the fabric could be concertina tucked (Chapter 10) or puckered (Chapter 6) and then cut and appliquéd in the desired location.

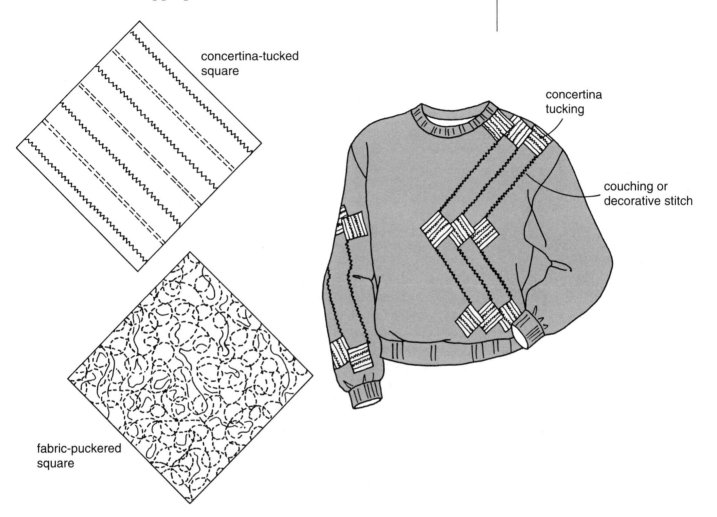

concertina-tucked square

concertina tucking

couching or decorative stitch

fabric-puckered square

Any time you visually want to join shapes or clusters of shapes together, considered cable stitching, couching, or dribbling, which is explained in Chapter 12. All of these techniques are quite effective and do not require a machine with fancy stitch patterns. If you do have decorative machine stitch patterns to choose from, stitching from shape to shape and repeating the stitch pattern can also do the job and add a lot of visual interest to the final creation.

BIOGRAPHIES

Margaret Lawtie

Jenny Anastas

Margaret Lawtie: From a very early age, I was exposed to the beauty of fashion sewing. My late mother was a very experienced dressmaker who had always strived for perfection. I would merely have to show her a rough sketch of my ideas and within a couple of days I would have a dress that would be the envy of my classmates at school. Throughout my life, I was able to build on the sewing skills I learned from my mother and in 1977 I applied for a position as a sewing machine demonstrator. This opportunity resulted in the awakening of my creative interests and eventually led to my desire to be a classroom instructor. With this expanding skill base, it opened up an exciting creative lifestyle. After some time, I was appointed area manager of Western Australia, a position I held for some years.

In 1989 I was offered a position with the Perth Sewing Center, that combined my talents, skills, and creative interests. I can proudly say that during this period, I have had the distinct privilege of meeting many talented and creative people. People such as Martha Pullen, a most inspirational lady who hails from the United States, and Kristen Dibbs, a fellow Australian, a most talented lady. Another Australian, Jenny Haskins, who has motivated me, is currently Pfaff Australia's national education and training manager. Also, the one who I am really indebted to is my own work colleague Jenny Anastas. Together we are responsible for the coordination of our company's creative workshops and the monthly Pfaff club meetings. Jenny was also instrumental in introducing me to the '84 Group, of which I am currently secretary. The aim of the '84 Group is to give mutual support among people working with educating others about contemporary embroidery in Perth, Western Australia. I feel so privileged to be associated with such dedicated people.

Last, but not least, I have had the wonderful opportunity of meeting Glenda Sparling and her husband Wesley. I am grateful to the Sparlings for recognizing my talents and for drawing upon them during the production of this book.

As you read *Wrapped in Fabriqué*™, may you experience the wonderful thrill of creating garments you will be proud to wear.

Jenny Anastas: I was born in Townsville, Queensland, Australia of Greek heritage and have spent most of my life in Perth, Western Australia. I am the wife of a medical general practitioner and have three sons.

I was taught at an early age by my grandmother and mother to knit, crochet, and hand embroider. Embroidery was my first love and I enjoyed crocheting as well. In my late teens, I broadened these interests to include dressmaking — although I have had no formal training in dressmaking, art, or machine embroidery.

In 1985, I became fascinated with appliqué and the techniques of creative machine embroidery. I then joined a newly formed group of contemporary machine embroiderers called the '84 Group, which is becoming well known in Australia. The '84 Group has had exhibitions in Perth as well as in London. Some of my work was included in these exhibitions. My colleagues and friends in the '84 Group encouraged me to put my creative talents into design and experimentation with many techniques.

I have worked seriously in this medium since 1985. Initially I began experimenting with creative appliqué and freehand machine stitching. I have done many commissioned works.

Since 1988, I have been working for Pfaff teaching the many varied techniques of machine embroidery and many other sewing techniques.

Over the last 5 years, I have won several prizes. The most recent achievement being winning first prize in an Australia and New Zealand competition for creative machine embroidery using preprogrammed stitches. (See color plate 15.)

I am happiest when creating designs and sewing at my machine. I love experimenting with colors, textures, fabrics, and threads and creating my own fabric.

Glenda Sparling

Glenda Sparling: I am truly one of those fortunate people who has been able to turn my hobby into a life long, enjoyable, and rewarding career. I first took home economics in junior high school and enjoyed every class. In those days, the first project was always an apron that you could wear in the cooking classes. I even enjoyed the *apron* project! As I was nearing the end of high school and having to make a career decision, I knew I wanted to take Home Economics at university. I did just that and four years later, I graduated with my under graduate degree in Home Economics from the University of Alberta, in Edmonton, Alberta.

I then taught Home Economics in an Alberta school district for 8 years. As a result of my success in the teaching profession, I had the opportunity to become the Home Economics consultant to the provincial government, a position of great challenge and reward. It was during this period that I finished a Master's Degree from the University of Oregon, married my husband Wesley, moved to Eugene, Oregon, and contemplated new career choices for myself in the sewing industry.

Initially I worked for Stretch and Sew as a corporate trainer in their Education Department. This led to my development of a fitting system marketed by Stretch and Sew and to a senior management position in their Research and Development department.

I ventured into my own business in 1982 with the formation of Ranita Corporation, a company specializing in pattern fitting, designing, and publishing. The challenges I faced in breathing life into our early business were monumental, however our success was made possible in great measure by the people we met who simply loved the great fitting Sure-Fit Designs™ patterns. From that challenging beginning in 1982, Ranita Corporation has expanded and established subsidiary companies in Canada and Australia. This gave me the opportunity to travel internationally to conduct seminars, shows, and classes. As a result, I have been able to realize my dream...to provide home seamstresses with practical ideas that result in stunning one-of-a-kind creations!

I hope that you, the reader, experience growth in your own creativity and enjoy doing these Fabriqué™ techniques and processes, as much as I enjoyed the creative challenge of experimenting with the ideas and writing this book.

RESOURCE LIST

For any Fabriqué™ project, having the right tools, equipment, and supplies is necessary for the accomplishing the process. To further assist you with achieving a successful project, as well as creative excellence, we have compiled a resource list of companies from which you may obtain the latest in tools, equipment, and supplies. If some of the items listed are not available in your geographic area, or if you want further information on where to obtain these items, please contact Ranita Corporation, P.O. Box 5698, Eugene, OR 97405-0698 TEL: (503) 344-0422 FAX: (503) 344-3944.

Not all these supplies are needed for every Fabriqué™ project. However, for your convenience, here is a comprehensive supply list compiled from all of the chapters. See the Specific Materials and Supplies list at the beginning of each chapter for items needed for that process only. If you need assistance to find these items, please contact Ranita Corporation.

- Cardboard dressmaker's cutting board, pin board, or foam core board
- Designer's Companion (small curved designing "ruler")
- Designing Stylus™/French Curve
- Disappearing fabric-marking pen
- Dressmaker's carbon and tracing wheel
- Fabric:
  Basic garment fabrics
  Douppioni silk
  Lamé
  Organza
  Satin
  Thai silk
  soft, drapable fabric
- Flat bed for sewing machine
- Knitting needle or wooden skewer
- Needles (sewing machine):
  Embroidery
  Metalfil
  Spring darning
  Twin (double)
  Variety of regular sizes
- Patterns
- Rotary cutter and cutting mat
- Rubber bands
- Scissors/Shears:
  Embroidery scissors
  Fabric shears
  Paper scissors

- Stabilizers:
  Embroidery hoops
  Fusible fleece
  Iron-on interfacing
  Iron-on stabilizer
  Liquid stabilizer
  Paper–backed, fusible webbing
  Tear–away stabilizer
  Vanishing muslin
  Water–soluble fabric
- T-square
- Teflon-coated appliqué mat (teflon pressing sheet)
- Thread:
  Elastic thread
  Heavy decorative bobbin thread (for example, Madeira's Glamour)
  Metallic Thread
  Rayon Thread
- Tracing Vellum
- Trims:
  Beads
  Braid
  Bugle beads
  Cord
  Lace
  Ribbons
  Sequins

American Resources:

Aardvark Adventures, Box 2449, Livermore, CA 94551. (800) 388-2687. *Glitz threads, beads, creative books. Catalog $2 (refundable on first order)*

Bernina of America, Inc., 3500 Thayer Ct., Aurora, IL 60504-6182. (708) 978-2500

Burda Patterns, Box 670628, Marietta, GA 30066. (800) 241-6887

Clotilde, Inc., 2 Sew Smart Way, Box 8031, Stevens Point, WI 54481-8031. (800) 772-2891

Coats & Clark, 30 Patewood Plaza, Suite 351, Greenville, SC 29615

Dritz Corp., P.O. Box 5028, Spartanburg, SC 29304. *Interfacings and other sewing notions.*

Elna, Inc., 7642 Washington Ave. S., Minneapolis, MN 55344.

G Street Fabrics, 12240 Wilkins Ave., Rockville, MD 20852. (800) 333-9191. *All fabrics mail order, custom service, free swatch service.*

Great Fit Patterns, 2229 N.E. Burnside, Suite 305, Gresham, OR 97030. (503) 665-3125. *Catalog $1.00*

Greenberg & Hammer, Inc., 24 W. 57th St., New York, NY 10019. (800) 955-5135. *Notions, patterns, silk threads, scissors, professional irons and more. Mail-order catalog, $10 minimum.*

J. & R Interfacings, c/o Dritz Corp., P.O. Box 5028, Spartanburg, SC 29304. *Interfacings and specialty fabrics.*

Jehlor Fantasy Fabrics, 730 Andover Park West, Seattle, WA 98188. (206) 575-8520. *Lamé, trims, beads, and sequins. Catalog $5 (refundable with order of $50 or more).*

June Tailor, Inc., P.O. Box 208, Richfield, WI 53076. (800) 844-5400. *Pressing and ironing equipment, rotary cutting boards and mats, appliqué mat.*

Kwik Sew Pattern Co., 3000 Washington Ave. North, Minneapolis, MN 55411. (800) 328-3953

M&J Trimming Company, 1008 6th Ave., New York, NY 10018. (212) 391-9072. *Huge selection of trims, braids, cords, and embellishments. Mail-order with $50 minimum.*

Madeira Marketing Ltd., 600 East 9th Street, Michigan City, IN 46360. (219) 873-1000

Nancy's Notions, Ltd., P.O. Box 683, Beaver Dam, WI 53916. (800) 833-0690. *Free catalog.*

National Thread & Supply Corp., Dept. A-202, 695 Red Oak Road, Stockbridge, GA 30281. (800) 331-7600, ext. A-202. *Pressing aids, notions.*

New Home Sewing Co., 100 Hollister Rd., Teterboro, NJ 07608. (201) 440-8080

Newark Dressmaker Supply, Box 20730, Lehigh Valley, PA 18002-0730. (215) 837-7500. *Mail-order source for almost all sewing supplies. Free catalog.*

Pellon Company Limited, Consumer Products Dept., 1040 Avenue of the Americas, New York, N.Y. 10018. (800) 223-5275 *Interfacings, Stitch & Tear.*

Pfaff American Sales Corp., 610 Winters Ave., Paramus, NJ 07653. (201) 262-7211

Sewing Emporium, 1079 Third Ave., Chula Vista, CA 91910. (619) 420-3490. *Notions and accessories. Catalog $4.95 (refundable on first order).*

Singer Sewing Co., 200 Metroplex Dr., Edison, NJ 08818.

So-Good, Inc., 28 W. 38th St., New York, NY 10018. (212) 398-0236. *Ribbons and trims.*

Staple Sewing Aids, 141 Lanza Ave., Garfield, NJ 07026. (800) 631-3820. *Interfacings.*

Stretch and Sew Patterns, P.O. Box 185, Eugene, OR 97440. (503) 726-9000

Sulky Threads, 3113 Broadpoint Dr., Harbor Heights, FL 33983. (813) 629-3199

Sure-Fit Designs™, P.O. Box 5698, Eugene, OR 97405. (503) 344-0422, FAX (503) 344-3944. *Dress, Pant, Shirt, Children's multi-size patterns, designing tools, Designing Stylus™, tracing vellum.*

Thai Silks, 252 State St., Los Altos, CA 94022. (800) 722-7455. *Variety of silks.*

The Fabric Carr, P.O. Box 32120, San Jose, CA 95152. (408) 929-1651. *Professional ironing supplies, sewing notions, books.*

Tinsel Trading Co., 47 W. 38th St., New York, N.Y. 10018. (212) 730-1030, FAX (212) 768-8823.*Antique gold and silver trims, real gold and silver threads.*

Treadleart, 25834 Narbonne Ave., Lomita, CA 90717. (310) 534-5122. *Decorative and utility machine threads, teflon pressing sheet, specialty feet. Catalog $3 (refundable with $20 purchase)*

VWS, Inc., 11750 Berea Road, Cleveland, OH 44111-1601. (216) 252-2047

Australian Resources:

Bernina, 15 Carrington Rd., Castle Hill, NSW 2154, (02) 8991188

Elna, 2 George Place, Artarmon, NSW 2064, (02) 4277511

Husquvarna, 647 Waverly Rd., Glen Waverly, Victoria 3150, (03) 566522

Janome, Unit 8, 1-15 Mills St., Cheltenham, Victoria 3192, (03) 5847622

Madeira Australia, 25-27 Izett St., Prahran, Victoria 3181, (03) 5294400

Perth Sewing Centre, Shop 20, Woodvale Blvd. Shopping Centre, Cnr. Whitford Ave & Trappers Drive, Woodvale, W.A. 6026 (09) 3095199 *Sewing machines and specialty items.*

Pfaff Australia Pty. Ltd., Unit 1, 13 Hoyle Ave., Castle Hill, NSW 2154, (02) 8946311

Singer, Unit 1, 13 Hoyle Ave., Castle Hill, NSW 2154, (02) 3997777

Sure-Fit Designs™ Pty. Ltd., P.O. Box 274, Kotara Fair, NSW 2289 (049) 562882

Bager, Bertel, *Nature as Designer,* Van Nostrand Reinhold, 1976.

Bakke, Karen, *The Sewing Machine as a Creative Tool,* Prentice-Hall, 1976.

Barker, Linda, *That Touch of Class/Machine Embroidery on Leather,* (c/o Treadleart, 25834 Narbonne Ave., Lomita, CA 90717).

Bennett, *Machine Embroidery with Style,* Madrona Publishers, 1980.

Better Homes & Gardens, *Creative Machine Stitchery,* Meredith, 1985.

Boyce, Ann, and Sandra L. Hatch, *Putting on the Glitz,* Chilton Book Co., 1991.

Boyce, Ann, *Appliqué The Ann Boyce Way,* Chilton Book Co., 1993.

Bray, Karen, *Machine Appliqué,* (21 Birch Dr., Walnut Creek, CA), 1978.

Brown, Pauline, *Embroidery, Skills Appliqué,* Merehurst, London, 1989.

Curran, Doreen, *The Magic of Free-Machine Embroidery,* Kangaroo Press, 1992.

Dibbs, Kristen, *The Fine Art of Machine Embroidery,* Simon Schuster, Australia, 1991.

Diethelm, Walter, *Visual Transformation,* Hastings House, 1982.

Fanning, Robbie, and Tony Fanning, *The Complete Book of Machine Embroidery,* Chilton Book Co., 1986.

Gattto, Joseph A., et al, *Exploring Visual Design,* Davis, 1978.

Graves, Maitland, *The Art of Color and Design,* McGraw-Hill, 1951.

Gray, Jennifer, *Machine Embroidery/Technique and Design,* Van Nostrand Reinhold, 1973.

Hanks, Kurt, et al, *Design Yourself!,* William Kaufmann, 1977.

Holt, Verna, *Verna's Machine Embroidery Series,* (3221 Joanne Way #B, Las Vegas, NV 89108), 1983.

Howard, Constance, *Inspiration for Embroidery,* BT Batsford/Charles T. Branford, 1966.

Johnson, Beryl, *Advanced Embroidery Techniques,* BT Batsford, 1983.

Landa, Robin, *An Introduction to Design,* Prentice-Hall, 1982.

Lee, Barbara, *Successful Machine Appliqué,* Yours Truly/Burdett, 1978.

Maier, Manfred, *Basic Principles of Design* (4 volumes), Van Nostrand Reinhold, 1977.

McGehee, Linda F., *Texture with Textiles, More Texture with Textiles.* Ghee's, 1993.

Meilach, Dona Z., et al, *How to Create Your Own Designs,* Doubleday, 1975.

Newman, Thelma, et al, *Sewing Machine Embroidery and Stitchery,* Crown, 1980.

Proctor, Richard M., and Jennifer F. Lew, *Surface Design for Fabric,* Univ. of Washington Press, 1984.

Reeder, S. Gail, *Creative Appliqué,* Willcraft Publishers (5093 Williamsport Dr., Norcross, GE 30071), 1983.

Ripley, Shirley R., *Decorate a Shirt, Creative Machine Embroidery* (2127 N. Sossaman, Mesa, AZ 85207), 1980.

Risley, Christine, *The Technique of Creative Embroidery,* Studio Vista, 1969.

Risley, Christine, *Machine Embroidery, A Complete Guide,* Studio Vista, 1973.

BIBLIOGRAPHY

Short, Eirian, *Embroidery and Fabric Collage,* Sir Isaac Pitman & Sons Ltd., 1967.

Singer, Margo and Mary Spyrou, *Textile Arts — Multicultural Traditions,* Chilton Book Co., 1990.

Strache, Wolf, *Forms and Patterns in Nature,* Pantheon Books, 1973.

Sulky of America, *Surface Design Concepts in Sulky,* A Sulky of America Publication, 1993.

Swift, Gay, *Machine Stitchery,* Charles T. Branford, 1974.

Thiel, Philip, *Visual Awareness and Design,* Univ. of Washington Press, 1981.

Thompson, Sue, *Decorative Dressmaking,* Rodale Press, 1985.

Tower, Libby, et al, *Elegant Way to Appliqué,* (P.O. Box 16800, Suite 180, Mesa, AZ 85202), 1984.

Wadsworth, John W., *Designs from Plant Forms,* Universe Books, 1910, 1977.

Wagner, Deb, and Esther Wagner, *Wagner's Sewing Machine Artistry,* (774 S. Dale St., Hutchinson, MN 55350), 1984.